FREE VIDEO FREE **FREE VIDEO**

CJBAT Essential Test Tips Video from Trivium Test Prep!

Dear Customer,

Thank you for purchasing from Trivium Test Prep! We're honored to help you prepare for your CJBAT exam.

To show our appreciation, we're offering a **FREE *CJBAT Essential Test Tips* Video by Trivium Test Prep**.* Our video includes 35 test preparation strategies that will make you successful on the CJBAT. All we ask is that you email us your feedback and describe your experience with our product. Amazing, awful, or just so-so: we want to hear what you have to say!

To receive your **FREE *CJBAT Essential Test Tips* Video**, please email us at 5star@ triviumtestprep.com. Include "Free 5 Star" in the subject line and the following information in your email:

1. The title of the product you purchased.
2. Your rating from 1 – 5 (with 5 being the best).
3. Your feedback about the product, including how our materials helped you meet your goals and ways in which we can improve our products.
4. Your full name and shipping address so we can send your **FREE *CJBAT Essential Test Tips* Video**.

If you have any questions or concerns please feel free to contact us directly at: 5star@ triviumtestprep.com.

Thank you!

- Trivium Test Prep Team

*To get access to the free video please email us at 5star@triviumtestprep.com, and please follow the instructions above.

CJBAT STUDY GUIDE

Comprehensive Review Book with Practice Exam
Questions for the Criminal Justice Basic Abilities Test
(Florida Law Enforcement Test Prep)

TABLE OF CONTENTS

INTRODUCTION   i

1 WRITTEN COMPREHENSION   1

Introduction..1

Topic and Main Idea 3

Supporting Details 5

Drawing Conclusions 6

The Author's Purpose and Point of View...7

Comparing Passages 9

Meaning of Words..............................10

Answer Key 13

2 WRITTEN EXPRESSION   15

Introduction 15

The Parts of Speech 16

Punctuation 18

Phrases 19

Clauses 19

Common Grammatical Errors 20

Vocabulary 26

Spelling 31

Answer Key 37

3 REASONING, SPATIAL ORIENTATION, AND MEMORIZATION   39

What is Reasoning? 39

Inductive Reasoning...........................39

Deductive Reasoning..........................42

Problem Sensitivity............................44

Spatial Orientation............................45

Information Ordering 47

Memorization....................................47

Answer Key 49

4 PRACTICE TEST   51

Written Comprehension.....................51

Written Expression 56

Inductive Reasoning..........................58

Deductive Reasoning..........................61

Information Ordering 67

Problem Sensitivity............................72

Spatial Orientation............................77

Memorization....................................80

Answer Key.......................................85

INTRODUCTION

Congratulations on choosing to take the Criminal Justice Basic Abilities Test (CJBAT)! By purchasing this book, you've taken an important step on your path to becoming a law enforcement officer in Florida.

This guide will provide you with a detailed overview of the CJBAT, so you know exactly what to expect on exam day. We'll take you through all the concepts covered on the exam and give you the opportunity to test your knowledge with practice questions. Even if it's been a while since you last took a major exam, don't worry; we'll make sure you're more than ready!

WHAT IS THE CJBAT?

The CJBAT is a comprehensive exam used to assess candidates aspiring to enter the field of law enforcement or corrections in the state of Florida. Any applicants to police or corrections academies in Florida must pass the CJBAT to begin training as officers. Most major police departments in Florida require the CJBAT, as does the Florida Highway Patrol Training Academy.

WHAT'S ON THE CJBAT?

The CJBAT tests candidates on language skills, reasoning, spatial orientation, and memorization. There are 120 multiple-choice questions on the test. Candidates have two hours and thirty minutes to respond to all the questions.

What's on the CJBAT?

QUESTION TYPE	NUMBER OF QUESTIONS
Written Comprehension	15
Written Expression	15
Inductive Reasoning	15
Deductive Reasoning	15
Information Ordering	15
Problem Sensitivity	15
Spatial Orientation	15
Memorization	15
2 hours and 30 minutes	120 questions

Written Comprehension

WRITTEN COMPREHENSION questions test your ability to understand written texts. You will be asked to identify details from reading passages or draw conclusions. There are fifteen Written Comprehension questions on the CJBAT.

Written Expression

WRITTEN EXPRESSION questions test your grammatical and writing skill. You may be asked about subject-verb agreement, spelling, or sentence structure. There are fifteen Written Expression questions on the CJBAT.

Reasoning

There are several types of reasoning questions on the CJBAT: Inductive Reasoning, Deductive Reasoning, Information Ordering, and Problem Sensitivity, with fifteen questions each.

INDUCTIVE REASONING questions ask you to draw conclusions from quantitative information provided in the forms of charts or graphs. Questions might ask about the impact of policies or certain trends over time. Applying your inductive reasoning skills using the information provided in the visual aids will allow you to answer the questions. There are fifteen Inductive Reasoning questions.

On DEDUCTIVE REASONING questions, you will be provided with a written excerpt from Florida State Law. Then, you will be presented with a situation related to that written material and asked a question about it. To find the correct answer, you will need to use the legal information provided to resolve the situation. Appropriate application of general rules to a specific situation is *deductive reasoning*. There are fifteen Deductive Reasoning questions on the CJBAT.

INFORMATION ORDERING questions ask you to place a series of statements into chronological or logical order. You will be presented with five or six statements out of order, and then you will choose the answer that places them in the correct order. There are fifteen Information Ordering questions on the test.

PROBLEM SENSITIVITY questions test your ability to understand if a situation is deteriorating or if something is likely to go wrong. In these questions, you will read a description of a situation, and determine what the issue is or how to resolve it. There are fifteen Problem Sensitivity questions on the test.

Spatial Orientation

SPATIAL ORIENTATION questions determine your ability to understand where you are located in relation to something else. On the exam, you will review maps and determine the fastest routes between locations, or where a vehicle or suspect has traveled. There are fifteen Spatial Orientation questions on the exam.

Memorization

MEMORIZATION questions test your observation skills. You will have two minutes to review a photograph or picture, and then you will be asked questions about details in the image. There are fifteen Memorization questions on the CJBAT.

SCORING

There are 120 questions in total on the CJBAT. You receive one point for each question you answer correctly; this is your raw score. That score is then converted into a scaled score ranging from 1 – 100. There is no guess penalty, so if you are not sure what the answer is to a question, you should guess. You might get it right and score another point.

A passing score on the CJBAT is determined by the agency or academy to which the candidate applies. That means different academies and agencies have different requirements. One department might require a score of 79; another might require an 85. Check with the academy or department you are interested in for details.

If you fail the CJBAT, you may take it up to three times in one year. You may not take the same version of the test you failed. Scores are valid for four years.

ADMINISTRATION AND TEST DAY

The CJBAT is administered by participating law enforcement agencies and academies. To register for the exam, you must directly contact the participating agency or academy where you are applying. You may take the CJBAT in a pencil-and-paper format or a computer-administered format.

On test day, arrive early. Check with the facility or participating agency to make sure you know what type of identification to bring (usually government-issued photo identification). Bring at least two sharpened No. 2 pencils. Personal belongings, cell phones, and other electronic, photographic, recording, or listening devices are not permitted in the testing center. Many testing centers offer lockers to secure your personal items, but you should check beforehand with the facility to be sure storage is available.

TIPS FOR TACKLING MULTIPLE-CHOICE QUESTIONS

The following tips assume you have a basic understanding of test taking: how to follow test proctor instructions, properly record answers, make sure the answer for the right question is recorded, and review an answer sheet before submitting it. If you do nothing else to prepare, learn these quick tips. They will help you focus your efforts and use your time wisely.

Handling Distractors

Distractors are the incorrect answer choices in a multiple-choice question. They "distract" you from the correct answer. Read and answer the question below:

> **Criminals are people who violate _____.**
>
> **A)** Penal Code 62
>
> **B)** civil procedure
>
> **C)** martial law
>
> **D)** criminal laws

The correct answer choice is D, criminal laws. The other, incorrect answer choices—the distractors—are designed to distract the inattentive test taker by "sounding" right or formal. While choices A and C may be partially correct—breaking a specific penal code (criminal) or martial (civilian-imposed military) law may be a crime—neither is the *best* answer choice.

Be sure to read the question for context and tone, and try to determine what is being asked. The preceding question asked for a general definition and used wording from the question as part of the correct answer. While a criminal might violate a *specific* penal code or martial law, generally, violations can be of *any* criminal law. Because criminals are guilty of crimes and *all* criminal laws involve or pertain to crime, choice D is the *best* answer.

Develop a Time Strategy

The examination is two and one-half hours, or 150 minutes, long. If you divide the time equally over the exam, you should have approximately one minute and fifteen seconds to answer each question. Pay attention to the time. Note the start and end time for each section prior to beginning. Make a goal to complete each question in one minute or less. One minute seems like a short amount of time, but it actually is not. You will likely complete most questions in less than thirty seconds. Develop your strategy such that you finish the easier questions quickly to allow more time to spend on the difficult questions.

Don't spend too much time on difficult questions. Mark them, skip them, and come back when you have time.

Focus on the Question

Read the question carefully. Words sometimes change meaning based on context. Context is the part of a communication that comes before or after a specific word or passage and provides clarity or meaning. Make sure you read and understand the question before selecting an answer. Read the following sentences:

> The police **arrested** Chad when he was eighteen years old.
>
> Chad is thirty-two years old, but his emotional development was **arrested** when he was eighteen years old.

The word *arrested* is used correctly in both sentences, but it has different meanings depending on the context.

Try to think of an answer before looking at the choices. This can keep you from being distracted by the incorrect answer choices and help you more easily identify the answer.

Correct is Not Always Best

Several answers could be *correct*, or close to correct, but you must choose the *best* answer choice. Beware of answer choices that are close to the correct answer but are merely distractions.

Use the Process of Elimination

Eliminate answer choices you know are incorrect. Choose your answer from the remaining choices.

For "All of the Above" and "None of the Above" answer choices, look for choices that include elements that break the "All" or "None" rule, such as a true element in a group of false elements or vice versa. If one element does not belong with the rest of the group's elements, then the answer cannot be *all*, or *none*, of the above.

Reread the question and remaining answers and select an answer choice.

ABOUT THIS GUIDE

This guide will help you master the most important test topics and develop critical test-taking skills. We have built features into our books to prepare you for your tests and increase your score. Along with a detailed summary of the test's format, content, and scoring, we offer an in-depth overview of the content knowledge required to pass the test. In the review you'll find sidebars that provide interesting information, highlight key concepts, and review content so that you can solidify your understanding of the exam's concepts. You can also test your knowledge with sample questions throughout the text and practice questions that reflect the content and format of the CJBAT. We're pleased you've chosen Trivium to be a part of your journey!

WRITTEN COMPREHENSION

INTRODUCTION

In the land of movies and television, law enforcement officers are rarely shown reading. Dirty Harry, John McClane, Horatio Caine, or Andy Sipowicz would be hard-pressed to pick up the penal code, case notes, or even a newspaper! But in the real world, shooting up the entire downtown area would cost the city and county millions of dollars in repair costs and civil suits. Turning your back on suspects to don sunglasses can get you fired, sued, or hurt. For police officers in real life, reading is a huge part of the job.

Law enforcement officers spend a considerable amount of time reading reports, case law, statutes, subpoenas, warrants, investigative notes, memos and policy changes, news reports about policing and the community, and more. Understanding what you read is paramount because it may dictate how you do the job.

You do not need to use outside knowledge on reading comprehension questions. Remember, the answer is located within the passage.

Misunderstanding what you read could cost you your job. Reading comprehension is one of the most important aspects of law enforcement. On the *Written Comprehension* section, the CJBAT tests applicants' reading comprehension abilities by presenting a passage to read, then asking several questions about the passage's content. The following information provides tips and tricks to improve your skills and navigate the reading comprehension section of the exam.

Reading for Understanding

Reading for understanding is different from reading for entertainment. Rather than simply skimming a passage for generalized information, the reader must dig more deeply into the text, make inferences and connections, and evaluate and interpret ideas and information. However, an integral part of reading comprehension is answering questions about the information. To be proficient at comprehension, readers must master several tasks while reading a particular passage:

DIFFERENTIATE FACT FROM OPINION. Many readers cannot tell the difference between fact and opinion. Contrary to popular belief, fact and opinion are not opposites; instead, they are differing types of statements. A **FACT** is a statement that can be proven by direct or objective evidence. Juries are called the "finders of fact" because they use the evidence presented to prove a statement. On the other hand, an **OPINION**, though it may be based in fact, is a statement established using belief or judgment and cannot be objectively proven true or false. Opinions are not necessarily wrong; they simply are not fact.

> Law enforcement officers often summarize in conversations. To ensure understanding, officers may repeat, in their own words, information a victim or suspect provides. The victim or suspect generally confirms or adjusts the restated information. To practice summarizing, after reading, take the information that is most important and restate it in it your own words.

DISTINGUISH BETWEEN WHAT IS IMPORTANT AND WHAT IS SIMPLY INTERESTING. When determining what is important in a passage, think about the main point and tone. What is the author trying to say? What is the main point? Information that tends to strengthen or weaken the main point is important. Information that does not strengthen or weaken the main point is simply interesting.

DETERMINE CAUSE-AND-EFFECT RELATIONSHIPS. Determine if there is a cause-and-effect relationship between pieces of information contained in the passage. Determining cause-and-effect relationships is important in comprehension as well as in establishing potential outcomes.

Look for words that show causal relationships, such as *because, since, therefore, thus,* and *so.*

COMPARE AND CONTRAST IDEAS AND INFORMATION. Connecting words often indicate transition within a passage. Understanding transitions can help keep you on track with the author's main point, rather than confusing you with opposing points of view in the passage. Look for words that show a shift in the author's position, such as *however, but, rather, in contrast,* and *although.*

DRAW CONCLUSIONS. Law enforcement officers regularly make inferences, draw conclusions, and make determinations based on information presented. After reading the passage, ask yourself:

- What judgments can be made based on the information provided?
- What evidence included in the passage supports that judgment?
- Are there other interpretations that can be made using the provided information and evidence?

Question Types

Reading comprehension tests generally use seven basic question types. They are explored in more detail in the chapter.

1. **WHAT'S THE MAIN POINT?** These questions ask you to identify the author's thesis or hypothesis. A question stem relating to this question type might ask, "The passage was primarily concerned with which of the following?" Check the thesis statement or conclusion for the answer to these types of questions.

2. **WHAT'S THE SUPPORTING IDEA?** These questions generally ask you to locate specific information. A question stem relating to this question type might ask, "The passage mentions each of the following EXCEPT…" You may need to reread the passage to find the answer. You might look for keywords in the answer choices to help steer you in the right direction.

> Read the passage carefully. Do not skim the passage. Read it two or three times to ensure you understand what the passage is communicating. Remember, this section is examining comprehension. Reading too quickly can cause you to miss important information.

3. **DRAWING INFERENCES.** Questions that require you to draw inferences often ask, "The passage implies which of the following?" The answer choices generally will closely imitate the text of the passage and rely upon specific facts provided.

4. **WHAT'S THE TONE?** These questions ask you to identify the author's attitude. Question stems generally ask, "The author's tone is best described as…"

5. **APPLY THE THEME TO OTHER CIRCUMSTANCES.** Questions requiring you to apply information from the passage to a similar situation often take the following form: "The author would most likely agree with which of the following?" There is no shortcut or trick to answering these question types. The key is identifying the heart of the passage and relating it to similar answer choices.

6. **LOGICAL REASONING.** This question style is the reverse of the "Application" question style. Logical reasoning questions ask you to take information from *outside* the passage and apply it to the passage to make determinations. An example of a logical reasoning question might be "Which of the following, if true, would most weaken the main point of the second paragraph?" Understanding the author's main point or argument and using your reasoning abilities to determine the value of answer choices will help you answer these questions.

> Read the passage before the question. Reading the question first can distract you from the main point of the passage. An error is more likely if you answer the question prematurely and without full understanding.

7. **RELATING DIFFERENT IDEAS.** These questions require you to determine the relationship between different ideas or parts of the passage. Questions are framed in a variety of ways, but they might ask how two paragraphs relate to each other or how an idea in one sentence contrasts with an idea later in the passage.

TOPIC AND MAIN IDEA

The **TOPIC** is a word or short phrase that explains what a passage is about. The **MAIN IDEA** is a complete sentence that explains what the author is trying to say about the topic. Generally, the **TOPIC SENTENCE** is the first (or near the first) sentence in a paragraph. It is a general statement that introduces the topic so the reader knows what to expect.

>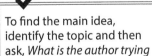
> To find the main idea, identify the topic and then ask, *What is the author trying to tell me about the topic?*

The SUMMARY SENTENCE, on the other hand, frequently (but not always!) comes at the end of a paragraph or passage because it wraps up all the ideas presented. This sentence summarizes what an author has said about the topic. Some passages, particularly short ones, will not include a summary sentence.

Table 1.1. Identifying Topic and Main Idea

Noise complaints are one of the most common calls received by police officers in cities and suburban areas. Close quarters and strong personalities make it more likely that neighbors will butt heads; the officer's job is to keep the peace. Usually, an officer can solve the problem by warning the offender. Most people will immediately turn down their music or end a late-night party when they find out they risk a hefty fine. On rare occasions, officers will issue citations for violating city ordinances or will arrest offenders for crimes like disorderly conduct.

TOPIC SENTENCE	Noise complaints are one of the most common calls received by police officers in cities and suburban areas.
TOPIC	noise complaints
SUMMARY SENTENCE	Close quarters and strong personalities make it more likely that neighbors will butt heads; the officer's job is to keep the peace.
MAIN IDEA	Officers respond to noise complaints, which are very common in crowded areas, to restore order.

Examples

1. **Topic**

   Police dogs usually work from six to nine years. K-9 officers have a variety of professional responsibilities: sniffing out explosives and narcotics, finding missing persons and human remains, and protecting officers. Many of them retire to live a comfortable life with their handlers, who know them better than anyone.

   What is the topic of the passage?

   (A) dog lifespan

   (B) police dogs

   (C) dog handlers

   (D) canine retirement

2. **Main Idea**

   The Battle of the Little Bighorn, commonly called Custer's Last Stand, was a battle between the Seventh Cavalry Regiment of the US Army and the combined forces of the Lakota, the Northern Cheyenne, and the Arapaho tribes. Led by war leaders Crazy Horse and Chief Gall and religious leader Sitting Bull, the allied tribes of the Plains Indians decisively defeated their US foes. Two hundred and sixty-eight US soldiers were killed, including Lieutenant Colonel George Armstrong Custer, two of his brothers, his nephew, his brother-in-law, and six Indian scouts.

   What is the main idea of this passage?

   (A) Most of Custer's family died in the Battle of the Little Bighorn.

   (B) The Seventh Cavalry Regiment was formed to fight Native American tribes.

   (C) Sitting Bull and George Custer were fierce enemies.

   (D) The Battle of the Little Bighorn was a significant victory for the Plains Indians.

SUPPORTING DETAILS

Statements that describe or explain the main idea are **SUPPORTING DETAILS**. Supporting details are often found after the topic sentence. They support the main idea through examples, descriptions, and explanations.

Authors may add details to support their argument or claim. **FACTS** are details that point to truths, while **OPINIONS** are based on personal beliefs or judgments. To differentiate between fact and opinion, look for statements that express feelings, attitudes, or beliefs that cannot be proven (opinions) and statements that can be proven (facts).

To find supporting details, look for sentences that connect to the main idea and tell more about it.

Table 1.2. Supporting Details and Fact and Opinion

Police academies have strict physical requirements for cadets. Cadets must pass fitness tests and train daily. As a result, some new recruits worry about their physical fitness before heading into the academy. Some graduates suggest focusing on core strength. Others believe that boxing is the best workout. We feel that cardiovascular activity is the most important exercise.

SUPPORTING DETAILS	Cadets must pass fitness tests and train daily.
FACT	Police academies have strict physical requirements for cadets.
OPINION	We feel that cardiovascular activity is the most important exercise.

Examples

3. Supporting Details

Increasingly, companies are turning to subcontracting services rather than hiring full-time employees. This provides companies with advantages like greater flexibility, reduced legal responsibility to employees, and lower possibility of unionization within the company. However, this has led to increasing confusion and uncertainty over the legal definition of employment. Courts have grappled with questions about the hiring company's responsibility in maintaining fair labor practices. Companies argue that they delegate that authority to subcontractors, while unions and other worker advocate groups argue that companies still have a legal obligation to the workers who contribute to their business.

Which detail BEST supports the idea that contracting employees is beneficial to companies?

(A) Uncertainty over the legal definition of employment increases.

(B) Companies still have a legal obligation to contractors.

(C) There is a lower possibility of unionization within the company.

(D) Contractors, not companies, control fair labor practices.

4. Fact and Opinion

An officer cited a motorist for reckless driving. The driver was performing unsafe maneuvers. The motorist was "doing donuts," rotating the vehicle. The officer observed this activity in a parking lot after dark. The officer wrote a citation. In addition, the vehicle was impounded.

Which statement from the passage is an opinion?

(A) An officer cited a motorist for reckless driving.

(B) The driver was performing unsafe maneuvers.

(C) The motorist was "doing donuts," rotating the vehicle.

(D) In addition, the vehicle was impounded.

DRAWING CONCLUSIONS

> Look for facts, character actions and dialogue, how each sentence connects to the topic, and the author's reasoning for an argument when drawing conclusions.

Readers can use information that is EXPLICIT, or clearly stated, along with information that is IMPLICIT, or indirect, to make inferences and DRAW CONCLUSIONS. Readers can determine meaning from what is implied by using details, context clues, and prior knowledge. When answering questions, consider what is known from personal experiences and make note of all information the author has provided before drawing a conclusion.

Table 1.3. Drawing Conclusions

When the Spanish-American War broke out in 1898, the US Army was small and understaffed. President William McKinley called for 1,250 volunteers to serve in the First US Volunteer Cavalry. The ranks were quickly filled by cowboys, gold prospectors, hunters, gamblers, Native Americans, veterans, police officers, and college students looking for an adventure. The officer corps was composed of veterans of previous wars. With more volunteers than it could accept, the army set high standards: all the recruits had to be skilled on horseback and with guns. Consequently, they became known as the Rough Riders.

QUESTION	Why are the volunteers named Rough Riders?
EXPLICIT INFORMATION	Different people volunteered, men were looking for adventure, recruits had to be extremely skilled on horseback and with guns due to a glut of volunteers.
IMPLICIT INFORMATION	Men had previous occupations; officer corps veterans worked with volunteers.
CONCLUSION DRAWN	The men were called Rough Riders because they were inexperienced yet enthusiastic to help with the war and were willing to put in extra effort to join.

Example

5. **Drawing Conclusions**

   "Swatting" is a dangerous practice. Someone falsely reports a crime in progress at a location to attract a large number of police to the site. The false crime usually involves hostages or a similar violent scenario, so police are prepared for confrontation. In fact, the term swatting is derived from the name for those police who specialize in such situations: the SWAT team, which carries high-caliber weapons and deploys flash bangs and tear gas. In a swatting incident, innocent citizens are shocked by a sudden police raid on their home. Likewise, police ready to face a violent perpetrator are surprised to find a family eating dinner or watching TV. The confusion caused by the false information and urgency of the raid make it very dangerous for all involved. Tragic outcomes are not uncommon.

   Which conclusion about the effects of swatting is most likely true?

   (A) Swatting is increasingly common, thanks to social media.

   (B) Swatting mostly occurs where there are large SWAT teams.

   (C) Swatting is usually harmless, though a waste of police time.

   (D) Swatting can result in injury or death to innocent citizens or officers.

THE AUTHOR'S PURPOSE AND POINT OF VIEW

The **AUTHOR'S PURPOSE** is his or her reason for writing a text. Authors may write to share an experience, to entertain, to persuade, or to inform readers. This can be done through persuasive, expository, and narrative writing.

PERSUASIVE WRITING influences the actions and thoughts of readers. Authors state an opinion, then provide reasons that support the opinion. **EXPOSITORY WRITING** outlines and explains steps in a process. Authors focus on a sequence of events. **NARRATIVE WRITING** tells a story. Authors include a setting, plot, characters, problem, and solution in the text.

Use the acronym P.I.E.S.—*persuade, inform, entertain, state*—to help you remember elements of an author's purpose.

Authors also share their **POINT OF VIEW** (perspectives, attitudes, and beliefs) with readers. Identify the author's point of view by word choice, details, descriptions, and characters' actions. The author's attitude, or **TONE**, can be found in word choice that conveys feelings or stance on a topic.

TEXT STRUCTURE is the way the author organizes a text. A text can be organized to show problem and solution, comparison and contrast, or even cause and effect. Structure of a text can give insight into an author's purpose and point of view. If a text is organized to pose an argument or advertise a product, it can be considered persuasive. The author's point of view will be revealed in how thoughts and opinions are expressed in the text.

Table 1.4. The Author's Purpose and Point of View

Officer ride-alongs are a great way for community members to get to know law enforcement officers. They are a valuable opportunity for students, journalists, community leaders, and those considering a career in law enforcement to learn more about the day-to-day experiences of police business. In a ride-along, you join an officer as he or she responds to calls, stops cars, and interacts with the public. Riders can ask questions and see the world from the perspective of a cop. Ride-alongs are a wonderful way for members of the public to learn about policing.

AUTHOR'S PURPOSE	persuade readers of the benefit of ride-alongs
POINT OF VIEW	advocates ride-alongs as "a great way for community members to get to know law enforcement officers"
TONE	positive, encouraging, pointing out the benefits of ride-alongs, using positive words like *great* and *wonderful*
STRUCTURE	descriptive: describes ride-alongs, giving specific examples to support the argument that they are valuable

Examples

6. **Author's Purpose**

   Several law enforcement departments in the United States have implemented sUAS (small unmanned aircraft systems), or drone programs. Drones provide intelligence, surveillance, and reconnaissance, known as ISR, helping inform decision-makers in reconstructing accidents and crime scenes, finding victims in search and rescue, and managing fire scenes. Local jurisdictions, such as the Los Angeles County Sheriff's Department, use drones. So do federal agencies like the US Border Patrol. What was once a military tool is becoming a valuable resource for law enforcement.

What is the purpose of this passage?

(A) to argue that drones are important for patrol

(B) to explain the history of drones in law enforcement

(C) to persuade readers that drone programs should be funded

(D) to describe how drones are used by law enforcement agencies

7. Point of View

Any law enforcement officer should expect to use force on the job at some point. Fortunately, officers have many nonlethal options for controlling a suspect or situation. Tasers, pepper spray, and batons are all effective for neutralizing a threat in many circumstances. Officers also train in basic ground and hand-to-hand tactics, though if possible they should avoid physical encounters for safety reasons. However, in certain situations officers must use their service pistols, which may result in a fatality.

Which of the following BEST describes what the author believes?

(A) Most forms of nonlethal force are effective, but not all.

(B) Lethal force should never be used because it is unethical.

(C) Officers should use nonlethal force if possible.

(D) Physical encounters should always be avoided.

8. Tone

Managing people is complicated in any field, and law enforcement is no different. Managers must balance administrative, financial, disciplinary, and policy responsibilities. Good managers also need to be aware of their subordinates' mental health in stressful fields like law enforcement. Recognizing the signs of stress, depression, substance abuse, and afflictions like post-traumatic stress disorder (PTSD) is an important skill for those who manage law enforcement personnel. The department can provide officers with support for mental wellness, improving their job performance and safety. The sooner a supervisor can spot symptoms, the faster the officer can receive assistance.

Which of the following best describes the author's attitude toward officers' mental health?

(A) dismissive

(B) sympathetic

(C) pitying

(D) angry

9. Text Structure

Increasingly, police departments require law enforcement officers to wear body cameras when they interact with members of the public. Some officers agree with this policy because the cameras provide protection against false complaints of police misconduct. Footage can exonerate police officers, proving their professionalism in situations. Other officers are cautious, worried that the cameras could limit officer discretion. Their concern is that supervisors might review and second-guess the officers' decisions during a call. What is undeniable is that the trend of body cameras is not going away as more jurisdictions across America adopt them.

What is the structure of this text?

(A) cause and effect

(B) order and sequence

(C) problem and solution

(D) compare and contrast

COMPARING PASSAGES

Sometimes readers need to compare and contrast two texts. After reading and identifying the main idea of each text, look for similarities and differences in the main idea, details, claims, evidence, characters, and so on.

When answering questions about two texts, first identify whether the question is about a similarity or a difference. Then look for specific details in the text that connect to the answers. After that, determine which answer choice best describes the similarity or difference.

> ⚠️ Use a Venn diagram, table, or highlighters to organize similarities and differences between texts.

Table 1.5. Comparing Passages

INTRANASALLY ADMINISTERED NALOXONE

Because even tiny amounts of the dangerous narcotic Fentanyl can result in overdose or death, many law enforcement officers carry the anti-overdose drug naloxone in case they encounter the frequently abused substance. Naloxone can be administered intranasally, allowing for rapid absorption into the bloodstream. The rescuer lays the victim on his or her back and sprays the medication into one nostril. The rescuer needs minimal training to administer naloxone in this way.

INJECTABLE NALOXONE

Naloxone, a medication that counteracts opioid overdose, is carried by many law enforcement officers in case of accidental contact with powerful narcotics like Fentanyl. Naloxone must be injected by trained first responders. Injectable naloxone is effective when the nasal cavity is damaged, for instance, if the victim has head trauma. Injectable naloxone is also used on detection dogs that have accidentally inhaled Fentanyl or another opioid and need a lower dose of naloxone than a human would.

SIMILARITIES (COMPARISON)	Both substances are used by law enforcement to fight accidental opioid overdose.
DIFFERENCES (CONTRAST)	Intranasally administered naloxone works rapidly and can be given by anyone. Injectable naloxone must be administered by a trained first responder and is more effective in specific situations.

Example

10. Comparing Passages

Self-Driving Cars: A Safer America

Self-driving cars, already present on our streets, are the wave of the future. They will make roads safer. Unlike human drivers, self-driving cars don't drink and drive, get lost in conversation, or fumble with phones. They can also be programmed to strictly adhere to the speed limit and traffic laws. That makes them the best bet for road and highway safety. Law enforcement officials will have more time to pursue violent criminals if they don't need to spend as much time monitoring highways for speeders and unsafe drivers.

<u>The Dangers of Autonomous Vehicles</u>

Many people are excited about autonomous vehicles, or self-driving cars, but they are risky machines. Already, several have been involved in deadly accidents, failing to brake for pedestrians or making inappropriate turns resulting in wrecks. Autonomous vehicles can malfunction; they occupy a gray area for law enforcement. What if an autonomous vehicle is speeding? How can highway patrol pull it over? What is the role for the traffic officer in an accident caused by a self-driving car? Who is accountable? There is no substitution for an experienced human driver with good judgment.

Which of these statements BEST compares the information in both texts?

(A) Autonomous vehicles are a social advantage.

(B) People are already using self-driving cars.

(C) Self-driving cars occupy a legal gray area.

(D) Officers will benefit from self-driving cars.

MEANING OF WORDS

To understand the meanings of unfamiliar words, use **CONTEXT CLUES**. Context clues are hints the author provides to help readers define difficult words. They can be found in words or phrases in the same sentence or in a neighboring sentence. Look for synonyms, antonyms, definitions, examples, and explanations in the text to determine the meaning of the unfamiliar word.

Sometimes parts of a word can make its meaning easier to determine. **AFFIXES** are added to **ROOT WORDS** (a word's basic form) to modify meaning. **PREFIXES** are added to the beginning of root words, while **SUFFIXES** are added to the ending. Divide words into parts, finding meaning in each part. Take, for example, the word *unjustifiable*: the prefix is *un–* (*not*), the root word is *justify* ("to prove reasonable"), and the suffix is *–able* (referring to a quality).

Use what you know about a word to figure out its meaning, then look for clues in the sentence or paragraph.

Another way to determine the meaning of unknown words is to consider their denotation and connotation with other words in the sentence. **DENOTATION** is the literal meaning of a word, while **CONNOTATION** is the positive or negative associations of a word.

Authors use words to convey thoughts, but the meaning may be different from a literal meaning of the words. This is called **FIGURATIVE LANGUAGE**. Types of figurative language include similes, metaphors, hyperboles, and personification.

Similes compare two things that are not alike with the words *like* or *as*. Metaphors are used to compare two things that are not exactly alike but may share a certain characteristic.

Hyperboles are statements that exaggerate something to make a point or to draw attention to a certain feature. Personification involves using human characteristics to describe an animal or object.

Table 1.6. Meanings of Words

Check fraud used to be a major crime, but today fewer people than ever use paper checks. Still, criminals continue to find ways to steal from consumers. Identity theft is a threat to all Americans as more people use credit cards and electronic financial applications than cash. Despite <u>encryption</u> techniques that protect personal details, computer hackers periodically uncover consumers' financial information in security breaches. Small-time thieves steal credit cards, use card skimmers at gas stations, or make fake cards with specialized machines.

CONTEXT CLUES	Techniques *protect* personal details; the details are still *uncovered* for criminal use.
AFFIXES	The prefix *en–* in *encryption* means *cause to*. The suffix *–ion* suggests an act or process.
ROOTS	The root of the word *encryption* is *crypt*, which means *hide* or *conceal*.
MEANING	*Encryption* means "the process of causing something to be hidden."

Examples

11. Context Clues

After a few high-profile missing-persons cases in the 1970s and 1980s, parents in many communities became concerned about "stranger danger." Families worried that their children would be <u>abducted</u>, taken by criminal outsiders. However, when a child goes missing, the perpetrator is usually someone the child knows. Family members make up the majority of perpetrators in cases of missing children. It is very rare that a child is kidnapped by a total stranger, though it can happen.

What does *abducted* mean as it is used in the passage?

(A) taken by criminal outsiders

(B) the perpetrator

(C) family members make up

(D) "stranger danger"

12. Root Words and Affixes

Unfortunately, automobile accidents happen. The good news is, most result in only minor damage to vehicles. Still, drivers are responsible for calling the police and reporting the incident, regardless of its severity. An officer will arrive to take the statement of each driver and survey the scene. The officer will closely examine the drivers' behavior and mannerisms to determine if their claims are <u>credible</u>. After all the evidence is collected, reviewed, and approved, the insurance company assigns blame to one party. The officer's role is key in this determination.

Based on affixes and context clues, what does *credible* mean?

(A) believable

(B) achievable

(C) likeable

(D) noticeable

13. Figurative Language

Nothing in the world is harder than waking up for a job you don't love. Who wants to drag themselves to work every day? That's why it's important to follow your passions. Many say that serving the public in law enforcement is more than just a job; it's a calling. Police officers risk their lives to serve and protect the public. It takes a certain kind of person to thrive in law enforcement.

Which type of figurative language is used in the second sentence?

(A) simile

(B) metaphor

(C) personification

(D) hyperbole

ANSWER KEY

1. **(B)** **Correct.** The topic of the passage is police dogs. The passage mentions how long they work, their handlers, and the usual retirement circumstances of police dogs as supporting ideas.

2. **(D)** **Correct.** The author writes that "the allied tribes...decisively defeated their US foes," and the remainder of the passage provides details to support this idea.

3. **(C)** **Correct.** The passage specifically presents this detail as one of the advantages of subcontracting services.

4. **(B)** **Correct.** The statement "The driver was performing unsafe maneuvers" is a judgment about the safety of the actions taken by the driver. The driver (or his attorney) might argue that his driving was safe.

5. **(D)** **Correct.** The passage states that swatting is dangerous because of confusion caused by false information and the nature of a violent raid. The sentence "Tragic outcomes are not uncommon" suggests that injury or death can happen.

6. **(D)** **Correct.** The text provides details on how drones are used and what departments use them.

7. **(C)** **Correct.** The author discusses many options for nonlethal force, using the word *fortunately* to show a preference for it. However, the author also allows that lethal force is sometimes necessary.

8. **(B)** **Correct.** The author states that "[t]he department can provide officers with support" and that supervisors should "be aware of their subordinates' mental health." By taking these positions, the author is being sympathetic and supportive of officers' mental health.

9. **(D)** **Correct.** In this text, two perspectives on body cameras are compared and contrasted.

10. **(B)** **Correct.** Both passages indicate that self-driving cars, or autonomous vehicles, are already in use.

11. **(A)** **Correct.** The phrase "taken by criminal outsiders" redefines the word *abducted* in the sentence.

12. **(A)** **Correct.** The root *cred* means *believe*. The words *evidence, reviewed*, and *approved* are context clues hinting that something needs to be believed and accepted.

13. **(B)** **Correct.** The writer uses the metaphor *drag*. No one literally drags himself or herself to work.

2

WRITTEN EXPRESSION

INTRODUCTION

Written and verbal communications are equally important in law enforcement. Writing accurate, clear, and concise memos, warrants, and police reports ensures that the information provided is as the officer intended. Unclear or confusing verbal communication can create misunderstanding and even danger if an officer is attempting to control a volatile situation. The same is true of written work. Wordy, incoherent, error-laden communications create confusion.

Clear and concise writing helps readers easily understand a message. In law enforcement, the last thing an officer wishes is for lawyers, juries, or the public to have to *guess* what he or she meant in a report or other written communication. Cases have been won and lost based on officer testimony related to a well-written or poorly written report.

Inspect the following two passages as an example of how wordiness and grammatical errors can confuse communication.

> **PASSAGE ONE**
>
> On Friday, August 17, 2014, about 1530 hours while working as a patrol officer in full uniform in Sector 2 of River City I heard over my car radio that Officer Smith had two people in front of Superior Court with warrants. I arrived at the Superior Court and met with Officer Smith. Officer Smith told me a woman, identified as Jane Johnson, and a man, identified as Ronald Jones, were at the courthouse. Jane and Ronald were at the court for a family hearing.
>
> A records check with River City Records and Warrants confirmed Jane had a misdemeanor warrant, and Ronald had a felony warrant, out of River City.
>
> Jane and Ronald were arrested without incident to answer for the warrant.

On Friday, August 17, 2014, about 1530 hours I contacted Jane Johnson and Ronald Jones in front of the River City Superior Court. Jane and Ronald were at the court for a family hearing. I had information both parties had active warrants for their arrest.

A records check with River City Records and Warrants confirmed Jane had an active misdemeanor warrant for her arrest and Ronald had an active felony warrant for his arrest, both issued by River City.

I arrested Jane and Ronald without incident to answer for their warrants.

Isn't it much easier to understand passage two? Are the sentences clear, concise, and grammatically correct, and do they contain all the necessary information? On the other hand, does passage one seem wordy and filled with grammatical errors? Is it clear or confusing? Unclear reports of search warrants could lead to poor investigations, arrests, and prosecutions.

The CJBAT tests common grammatical mistakes. Knowing the rules of grammar, mechanics, and sentence structure will help you choose the correct answer on the CJBAT. Furthermore, avoiding common errors can help add clarity to your written communication. We review the basics and common mistakes in this chapter.

The CJBAT also tests spelling. Two sections of this chapter focus on building your vocabulary, determining the meaning of unfamiliar words, and reviewing spelling rules.

THE PARTS OF SPEECH

NOUNS are the words that describe people, places, things, and ideas. The subject of a sentence is typically a noun. For example, in the sentence "The station was very clean," the subject, *station*, is a noun; it is a place.

Nouns have several subcategories: common nouns (*chair, car, house*), proper nouns (*Julie, David*), noncountable nouns (*money, water*), and countable nouns (*dollars, cubes*), among others. There is much crossover among these subcategories (for example, *chair* is both common and countable), and other subcategories do exist.

SINGULAR PRONOUNS
• I, me, my, mine
• you, your, yours
• he, him, his
• she, her, hers
• it, its
PLURAL PRONOUNS
• we, us, our, ours
• they, them, their, theirs

PRONOUNS replace nouns in a sentence or paragraph, allowing a writer to achieve a smooth flow throughout a text by avoiding unnecessary repetition. While there are countless nouns in the English language, there are only a few types of pronouns. Take the sentence "Sam stayed home from school because Sam was not feeling well." The noun *Sam* appears twice in the same sentence. Instead, the pronoun *he* can be used to stand in for *Sam*: "Sam stayed home from school because he was not feeling well."

VERBS express action (*run, jump, play*) or state of being (*is, seems*). Verbs that describe action are **ACTION VERBS**, and those that describe being are **LINKING VERBS**.

ACTION: My brother <u>plays</u> tennis.

LINKING: He <u>is</u> the best player on the team.

ADJECTIVES provide more information about a noun in a sentence. Take the sentence "The boy hit the ball." If you want your readers to know more about the noun *boy*, you could use an adjective to describe him: *the little boy, the young boy, the tall boy*.

ADVERBS describe verbs, adjectives, and even other adverbs. For example, in the sentence "The doctor had recently hired a new employee," the adverb *recently* tells us more about how the action *hired* took place.

> ⚠️ Participles are nouns or adjectives formed by adding *–ed* or *–ing* to a verb.
>
> <u>Seated</u> politely, Ron listened to his friend's boring story.
>
> Maya petted the <u>sleeping</u> cat.

PREPOSITIONS express the location of a noun or pronoun in relation to other words and phrases described in a sentence. For example, in the sentence "The nurse parked her car in a parking garage," the preposition *in* describes the position of the car in relation to the garage. Together, the preposition and the noun that follow it are called a PREPOSITIONAL PHRASE. In this example, the prepositional phrase is *in a parking garage*.

CONJUNCTIONS connect words, phrases, and clauses. INTERJECTIONS, like *wow* and *hey*, express emotion and are most commonly used in conversation and casual writing.

Examples

1. Which of the following lists includes all the nouns in the following sentence?

   I have lived in Minnesota since August, but I still don't own a warm coat or gloves.

   (A) coat, gloves

   (B) I, coat, gloves

   (C) Minnesota, August, coat, gloves

   (D) I, Minnesota, August, warm, coat, gloves

2. Which of the following lists includes all the adjectives in the following sentence?

   The new chef carefully stirred the boiling soup and then lowered the heat.

   (A) new, boiling

   (B) new, carefully, boiling

   (C) new, carefully, boiling, heat

   (D) new, carefully, boiling, lowered, heat

3. Choose the word that best completes the sentence.

   Her love _____ blueberry muffins kept her coming back to the bakery every week.

   (A) to

   (B) with

   (C) of

   (D) about

PUNCTUATION

The basic rules for using the major punctuation marks are given in the table below.

Table 2.1. Using Punctuation

PUNCTUATION	PURPOSE	EXAMPLE
Period	Ending sentences	Periods go at the end of complete sentences.
Question mark	Ending questions	What's the best way to end a sentence?
Exclamation point	Ending sentences that show extreme emotion	I'll never understand how to use commas!
Comma	Joining two independent clauses (always with a coordinating conjunction)	Commas can be used to join clauses, but they must always be followed by a coordinating conjunction.
	Setting apart introductory and nonessential words and phrases	Commas, when used properly, set apart extra information in a sentence.
	Separating items in a list	My favorite punctuation marks include the colon, semicolon, and period.
Semicolon	Joining together two independent clauses (never used with a conjunction)	I love exclamation points; they make sentences seem so exciting!
Colon	Introducing a list, explanation, or definition	When I see a colon, I know what to expect: more information.
Apostrophe	Forming contractions	It's amazing how many people can't use apostrophes correctly.
	Showing possession	Parentheses are my sister's favorite punctuation; she finds commas' rules confusing.
Quotation marks	Indicating a direct quote	I said to her, "Tell me more about parentheses."

Examples

4. Which of the following sentences contains an error in punctuation?

   (A) I love apple pie! John exclaimed with a smile.

   (B) Jennifer loves Adam's new haircut.

   (C) Billy went to the store; he bought bread, milk, and cheese.

   (D) Alexandra hates raisins, but she loves chocolate chips.

5. Sam, do you want to come with us for dinner_

   Which punctuation mark correctly completes the sentence?

   (A) .

   (B) ?

   (C) ;

   (D) :

PHRASES

Understanding subjects and predicates is key to understanding what a phrase is. The SUBJECT is what the sentence is about; the PREDICATE contains the verb and its modifiers.

> The nurse at the front desk will answer any questions you have.
>
> SUBJECT: the nurse at the front desk
>
> PREDICATE: will answer any questions you have

A PHRASE is a group of words that communicates only part of an idea because it lacks either a subject or a predicate. Phrases can begin with prepositions, verbs, nouns, or participles.

> PREPOSITIONAL PHRASE: The dog is hiding under the porch.
>
> VERB PHRASE: The chef wanted to cook a different dish.
>
> NOUN PHRASE: The big red barn rests beside the vacant chicken house.
>
> PARTICIPIAL PHRASE: Walking quietly, she tried not to wake the baby.

Example

6. Identify the type of phrase underlined in the following sentence:

   The experienced paraprofessional worked independently with the eager students.

   (A) prepositional phrase
   (B) noun phrase
   (C) verb phrase
   (D) participial phrase

CLAUSES

CLAUSES contain both a subject and a predicate. They can be either independent or dependent. An INDEPENDENT (or main) CLAUSE can stand alone as its own sentence.

> The dog ate her homework.

DEPENDENT (or subordinate) CLAUSES cannot stand alone as their own sentences. They start with a subordinating conjunction, relative pronoun, or relative adjective, which will make them sound incomplete.

> Because the dog ate her homework

Clauses can be joined together to create more complex sentences. COORDINATING CONJUNCTIONS join two independent clauses, and SUBORDINATING CONJUNCTIONS join an independent to a dependent clause.

Table 2.2. Conjunctions

Coordinating	*for, and, nor, but, or, yet, so (FANBOYS)*	The nurse prepared the patient for surgery, <u>and</u> the doctor performed the surgery.
Subordinating	*after, although, because, if, since, so that, though, until, when, while*	She had to ride the subway <u>because</u> her car was being serviced.

Example

7. Choose the word that best completes the sentence.

Christine left her house early on Monday morning, _____ she was still late for work.

(A) but

(B) and

(C) for

(D) or

COMMON GRAMMATICAL ERRORS

Pronoun-Antecedent Agreement

Pronouns must agree with their ANTECEDENTS (the words they replace) in number; however, some pronouns also require gender agreement (*him, her*). PRONOUN-ANTECEDENT AGREEMENT rules can be found below:

1. Antecedents joined by *and* typically require a plural pronoun.
   The <u>children and their dogs</u> enjoyed <u>their</u> day at the beach.
   If the two nouns refer to the same person, a singular pronoun is preferable.
   <u>My best friend and confidant</u> still lives in <u>her</u> log cabin.

2. For compound antecedents joined by *or*, the pronoun agrees with the nearer or nearest antecedent.
   Either the resident mice <u>or the manager's cat</u> gets <u>itself</u> a meal of good leftovers.

3. When indefinite pronouns function in a sentence, the pronoun must agree with the number of the indefinite pronoun.
   <u>Neither</u> student finished <u>his or her</u> assignment.
   <u>Both</u> students finished <u>their</u> assignments.

4. When collective nouns function as antecedents, the pronoun choice will be singular or plural depending on the function of the collective.
   The <u>audience</u> was cheering as <u>it</u> rose to <u>its</u> feet in unison.
   Our <u>family</u> are spending <u>their</u> vacations in Maine, Hawaii, and Rome.

5. When *each* and *every* precede the antecedent, the pronoun agreement will be singular.
   <u>Each and every man, woman, and child</u> brings unique qualities to <u>his or her</u> family.
   <u>Every creative writer, technical writer, and research writer</u> is attending <u>his or her</u> assigned lecture.

How would you complete the following sentence? "Every boy and girl should check _____ homework before turning it in." Many people would use the pronoun *their*. But since the antecedent is "every boy and girl," technically, the correct answer would be *his or her*. Using *they* or *their* in similar situations is increasingly accepted in formal speech, however. It is unlikely that you will see questions like this on the CJBAT, but if you do, it is safest to use the technically correct response.

Example

8. In which of the following sentences do the nouns and pronouns NOT agree?
    (A) After we walked inside, we took off our hats and shoes and hung them in the closet.
    (B) The members of the band should leave her instruments in the rehearsal room.
    (C) The janitor on duty should rinse out his or her mop before leaving for the day.
    (D) When you see someone in trouble, you should always try to help them.

Vague or Unclear Pronouns

A vague or unclear reference is generally the result of a PRONOUN ERROR. Pronoun errors occur when it is not clear what the antecedent of a pronoun is—the word it replaces. In the first sentence below, it is difficult to determine whose notes the officer gave to the Assistant District Attorney. Do the notes belong to the officer or to the ADA? The antecedent of the pronoun *his* is unclear. To improve this sentence, be sure the pronoun refers to only one antecedent noun.

> WRONG: Officer Lane gave Assistant District Attorney Poole <u>his</u> notes.
>
> CORRECT: Officer Lane gave <u>his</u> notes to Assistant District Attorney Poole.

Another way to ensure clarity in writing is to avoid using pronouns to refer to an implied idea; it is better to state the idea explicitly. In the sentence below, the writer misuses the pronoun *it*. The reader might be confused: did jury deliberation take a long time, or did the process of the trial take a long time? To improve this sentence, the writer should state the idea explicitly, avoiding a pronoun altogether.

> WRONG: The jury reached a verdict in the defendant's case, but <u>it</u> took a long time.
>
> CORRECT: The jury reached a verdict in the defendant's case, but <u>the deliberations</u> took a long time.

Example

9. Choose the more clearly written sentence.
    (A) John said he and Frank were fighting when he was shot.
    (B) John said he and Frank were fighting when Frank was shot.

Subject-Verb Agreement

Verbs are conjugated to indicate PERSON, which refers to the point of view of the sentence. First person is the speaker (*I, we*); second person is the person being addressed (*you*); and third person is outside the conversation (*they, them*). Verbs are also conjugated to match the NUMBER (singular or plural) of their subject. HELPING VERBS (*to be, to have, to do*) are used to conjugate verbs. An unconjugated verb is called an INFINITIVE and includes the word *to* in front of it (*to be, to break*).

Table 2.3. Verb Conjugation (Present Tense)

PERSON	SINGULAR	PLURAL
First person	I give	we give
Second person	you give	you (all) give
Third person	he/she/it gives	they give

Verbs must agree in number with their subjects. (In some other languages, such as Spanish, verbs must also agree with their subjects in gender.) SUBJECT-VERB AGREEMENT rules follow:

1. Singular subjects agree with singular verbs; plural subjects agree with plural verbs.
    The girl walks her dog.
    The girls walk their dogs.

2. Compound subjects joined by *and* typically take a plural verb unless they are considered one item.
    Correctness and precision are required for all good writing.
    Macaroni and cheese makes a great snack for children.

3. Compound subjects joined by *or* or *nor* agree with the nearer or nearest subject.
    Neither I nor my friends are looking forward to our final exams.
    Neither my friends nor I am looking forward to our final exams.

4. All singular indefinite pronouns agree with singular verbs.
    Neither of the students is happy about the play.
    Each of the many cars is on the grass.
    Every one of the administrators speaks highly of Officer Larkin.

5. All plural indefinite pronouns agree with plural verbs.
    Several of the students are happy about the play.
    Both of the cars are on the grass.
    Many of the administrators speak highly of Officer Larkin.

6. Some of the singular indefinite pronouns (*all, most, some, more, any*) change agreement depending on the object of the preposition.
    All of the pie is gone.
    All of the pies are gone.
    Some of the bucket is dirty.
    Some of the buckets are dirty.

7. Collective nouns agree with singular verbs when the collective acts as one unit. Collective nouns agree with plural verbs when the collective acts as individuals within the group.

The jury announces its decision after sequestration. (*They act as one unit.*)

The jury make phone calls during their break time. (*They act as individuals.*)

8. Nouns that are plural in form but singular in meaning will agree with singular verbs.

   Measles is a painful disease.

   Sixty dollars is too much to pay for that book.

9. Singular verbs come after titles, business corporations, and words used as terms.

   "Three Little Kittens" is a favorite nursery rhyme for many children.

   General Motors is a major employer for the city.

Ignore words between the subject and the verb when trying to match a subject and verb:

The new library ~~with its many books and rooms~~ fills a long-felt need.

Example

10. Which of the following sentences contains a subject-verb error?

    (A) The witness and her mother are asked to remain seated.

    (B) Some of the officers at the station is planning to stay late.

    (C) My partner and I are happy with the new schedule.

    (D) The department is hiring for many new positions this year.

Verb Tense Agreement

Verbs are also conjugated to indicate TENSE, or when the action has happened. Actions can happen in the past, present, or future. Tense also describes over how long a period the action took place.

- **SIMPLE** verbs describe general truths or something that happened once.

- **CONTINUOUS** verbs describe an ongoing action.

- **PERFECT** verbs describe repeated actions or actions that started in the past and have been completed.

- **PERFECT CONTINUOUS** verbs describe actions that started in the past and are continuing.

Table 2.4. Verb Tenses

TENSE	PAST	PRESENT	FUTURE
Simple	I gave her a gift yesterday.	I give her a gift every day.	I will give her a gift on her birthday.
Continuous	I was giving her a gift when you got here.	I am giving her a gift; come in!	I will be giving her a gift at dinner.
Perfect	I had given her a gift before you got there.	I have given her a gift already.	I will have given her a gift by midnight.
Perfect continuous	Her friends had been giving her gifts all night when I arrived.	I have been giving her gifts every year for nine years.	I will have been giving her gifts on holidays for ten years next year.

The verb tenses in a sentence must agree with each other and with the other information provided in the sentence. Pay attention to words like *before, after, tomorrow, yesterday, then,* and *next,* which describe when in time events occurred.

> **WRONG:** After he changed clothes, the officer will be ready to go home.
> **CORRECT:** After he changed clothes, the officer was ready to go home.

In the example above, the introductory phrase describes an action that was completed in the past (*he changed*), so the rest of the sentence should also be in the past (*was ready*).

Example

11. Which verb phrase best completes the sentence?

By this time tomorrow, we _____ in New York.

(A) will have arrived

(B) have arrived

(C) arrive

(D) was arriving

Comparing Adjectives and Adverbs

The suffix *−er* is used when comparing two things, and the suffix *−est* is used when comparing more than two. Adjectives longer than two syllables are compared using *more* (for two things) or *most* (for three or more things).

> Anne is taller than Steve, but Steve is more coordinated.
>
> Of the five brothers, Billy is the funniest, and Alex is the most intelligent.

More and *most* should NOT be used in conjunction with *−er* and *−est* endings.

> **WRONG:** My most warmest sweater is made of wool.
> **CORRECT:** My warmest sweater is made of wool.

Example

12. Which of the following sentences contains an adjective error?

(A) The new red car was faster than the old blue car.

(B) Reggie's apartment is in the tallest building on the block.

(C) The slice of cake was tastier than the brownie.

(D) Of the four speeches, Jerry's was the most long.

Misplaced Modifiers

A **MODIFIER** is a word or phrase—like an adjective—that adds detail to a sentence. Adjectives, adverbs, and modifying phrases should be placed as close as possible to the word they modify. **MISPLACED MODIFIERS** can create confusing or nonsensical sentences.

> **WRONG:** Running down the alley, the siren sounded and the police officer knew backup had arrived.
>
> **CORRECT:** Running down the alley, the police officer heard the siren and knew backup had arrived.

In the first example above, the phrase "running down the alley" looks like it is modifying "the siren." For clarity, it should be placed next to "the police officer," the noun it modifies.

> **WRONG:** Describing the crime, the jury listened to the prosecutor deliver his opening statement.
>
> **CORRECT:** The jury listened to the prosecutor deliver his opening statement describing the crime.

In this example, the phrase "describing the crime" is first placed next to the word "jury," making it seem like the jury is describing the crime. To fix the sentence, the modifier should be moved so it is clear that the prosecutor is describing the crime.

Example

13. Choose the more clearly written sentence.

(A) During police contacts, failure to follow directions is often the cause of officer uses of force.

(B) During police contacts, failure to follow directions often is the cause of officer uses of force.

Sentence Fragments

A sentence fragment occurs when a group of words is followed by a period but does not form a complete sentence or thought. A sentence fragment can be corrected by turning it into a complete sentence that has at least one independent clause.

> **WRONG:** Because he was tired of presiding over cases involving the same criminals in his courtroom.
>
> **CORRECT:** The judge left the bench because he was tired of presiding over cases involving the same criminals in his courtroom.

Example

14. Choose the more clearly written sentence.

(A) The suspect robbed an elderly woman and then fled the scene in a red sedan heading northbound on Eighth Avenue.

(B) The suspect robbed an elderly woman and then fled the scene in a red sedan. Heading northbound on Eighth Avenue.

Run-on Sentences

A **RUN-ON SENTENCE** is two or more complete sentences not separated by appropriate punctuation, such as a comma, period, or semicolon. For example, the following is a run-on sentence: "Jack shot his friend Mark over a pool game, Jack was mad because he thought Mark was cheating."

Be sure to separate each complete thought with proper punctuation. Applying this rule changes the preceding sentence: "Jack shot his friend Mark over a pool game. Jack was mad because he thought Mark was cheating."

Example

15. Choose the more clearly written sentence.

    (A) Jane broke into the house intending to steal items to exchange for drugs she activated the alarm and ran away.

    (B) Jane broke into the house intending to steal items to exchange for drugs. She activated the alarm and ran away.

Vocabulary

Vocabulary is a collection of words used or known in language. Possessing a large vocabulary can help you better understand communications. It can improve your ability to determine context and add clarity to the written or spoken word. Law enforcement vocabulary can be very technical, but it also contains many commonly used words. The vocabulary section of the CJBAT measures ability to understand and appropriately use *common* words.

On the CJBAT, each question is structured as one sentence with a word underlined. The answer choices list alternative words to replace the underlined word. You must choose the word that most closely matches the meaning of the underlined word.

Developing a large vocabulary takes time and practice; it cannot be done overnight. However, studying commonly used words and their synonyms can help. Synonyms are words that share the same or nearly the same meaning as other words. Understanding word roots, prefixes, suffixes, and how they affect words can also help you determine the meaning of unfamiliar words based on the word's structure.

Root Words

A ROOT WORD is the base of a word. It comes after a prefix or before a suffix. In English, many root words come from ancient Greek and Latin. Root words hold meaning and can stand alone as words. Learning to recognize common root words can help you build your vocabulary and make educated guesses about unfamiliar words. It can also help improve your ability to comprehend various types of communications.

Table 2.5 lists some common root words, their meanings, and examples.

Table 2.5. Common Root Words

ROOT	MEANING	EXAMPLES
actus, act	drive, lead, act	active, action, activate, react
acurer	to sharpen	acute, acumen, acuity
agon	contest, struggle	antagonist, agony
ambi	both	ambiguous, ambidextrous
anthropo	man, human, humanity	anthropologist, philanthropist
aqua	water	aquarium, aquatic
arbit	judge	arbitrary, arbitration
archos, arch	chief, first, rule	monarch, archangel, anarchy
aud	to hear	audience, audible, auditory
auto	self	autobiography, autograph, autoimmune, automobile

ROOT	MEANING	EXAMPLES
bene	good	benevolent, beneficial
bio	life	biology, biography
capere, cip, cept	take, seize	captive, capture, captivate, intercept
cedere, ced	to go, yield	recede, precede, exceed, predecessor
chron	time	chronological, chronic, synchronize
circum	around	circumference, circumvent, circumscribe
clino, clin	lean, slant	incline, decline, inclination, recline
contra, counter	against	contradict, contrary, counteract
cred	believe	creed, incredible
crit	judge	criticize, critical
crypto, crypt	hide, conceal	cryptic, cryptogram, encryption
dict	to say	dictation, dictate, predict
duc, duct	to lead	conduct, induce, induct
dyna	power	dynamic, dynamite, dynamo
dys	bad, hard, unlucky	dysfunctional, dyslexic, dystopia
equ	equal, even	equidistant, inequity, equivalent, equitable
errare, err, errat	wander, go astray	errant, err, erratic, aberration
fac	to do, to make	factory, manufacture, artifact
finis, fin	end, limit	final, definite, infinite
form	shape	conform, reform
fort	strength	fortitude, fortress, fortify, comfort
fract	to break	fracture, fraction
gno, gnos	know	diagnosis, ignore, incognito, cognitive
gram	something written	telegram, diagram, grammar
graph	writing	graphic, autograph
gravis, grav, griev	heavy, serious	grave, grievance, grievous, aggravate, gravity
hetero	different	heteronym, heterogeneous
homo	same	homonym, homogenous
hydro	water	hydrate, dehydrate, hydraulic
hypo	below, beneath	hypothermia, hypothetical, hypoglycemic
ject	throw	eject, project, reject
jud	judge	judicial, prejudice
jus, jur, just	right, law, oath	abjure, perjury, conjure, jury, jurisprudence
juven	young	juvenile, rejuvenate
mal	bad	malfeasance, malevolent, malcontent
mater	mother	maternal, maternity
meter, metr	measure	thermometer, perimeter, metric
micro	small	microbe, microscope, microchip

Table 2.5. Common Root Words (continued)

ROOT	MEANING	EXAMPLES
mis, miso	hate, wrong	misanthrope, misogyny, misbehave
mono	one	monologue, monotonous, monotheism
morph	form, shape	morphology, metamorphosis
mort	death	mortal, mortician, immortal
multi	many	multimedia, multiple, multiply, multicolored
nym	name	antonym, synonym, homonym
onus, oner	burden	onerous, onus, exonerate
opsis, optic	sight, eye, view	optical, synopsis
pater	father	paternal, paternity
phil	love	philanthropist, philosophy
phobia	fear	claustrophobia, acrophobia, phobic
phon	sound	cacophony, phonetic, symphony
photo, phos	light	photograph, photogenic, phosphorous
placaere	appease	placate, placid
port	to carry	portable, transportation, export
pretiare, prec	to value	precious, deprecation, depreciation, appreciation
pseudo	false	pseudonym, pseudoscience
psycho	soul, spirit	psychology, psychic, psychotic
rupt	to break	bankrupt, disrupt, erupt
scope	to watch, see	microscope, telescope
scrib, scribe	to write	inscribe, prescribe, describe
sect, sec	to cut	bisect, section, intersect, dissect
sentire, sent	to feel, perceive	consent, resent, sentient, sentiment
skep, scop	examine	skeptical, scope
spect	to look	inspect, spectator, circumspect, retrospective
struct	to build	construct, destruct, restructure, infrastructure
tacere, tac, tic	to be silent	tacit, taciturn, reticent
techno	art, science, skill	technique, technology
tele	far off	television, telephone, teleport
tendere	stretch	extend, tend, distend
terrere, terr	frighten	deter, terror, terrorism
therm	heat	thermal, thermometer, thermos
thesis	position	synthesis, hypothesis
venire, veni, ven	come, move toward	convention, contravene, intervene
vid, vis	to see	video, envision, evident, vision
voc	to call	voice, vocalize, advocate
zelos	ardor, passion	zeal, zealous, zealot

Prefixes

PREFIXES are sets of letters that are added to the beginning of a word. Adding a prefix to a word can change its meaning. For instance, if you take the root word *jud*, which means *judge*, and add the prefix *pre–*, which means *before*, you create the word *prejudice*, which means to prejudge.

Prefixes cannot stand on their own as words, but they do hold meaning. Learning to recognize common prefixes builds vocabulary and helps readers make educated guesses about unfamiliar words. It can also help improve reading comprehension in general.

Table 2.6 lists some common prefixes, their meanings, and examples.

Table 2.6. Common Prefixes

PREFIX	MEANING	EXAMPLES
ambi–, amb–	around, on both sides	ambiguous, ambivalent
anti–	against, opposite	anticlimactic, antiseptic
bi–	two	bicycle, bifocals, bilingual
circum–, circa–	around, about	circumference, circadian, circumvent
com–, con–	with	communicate, convince
contra–	against	contradict, contrary, contravene
de–	reduce, remove	devalue, decelerate, decompose
di, dis–	not, opposite of	discontinue, disappear, discover, digress
en–, em–	cause to, into	enact, empower, embrace, enclose
fore–	before, front of	foreshadow, forebear
il–, im–, in–, ir–	not, without	illegal, impossible, invalidate, irresponsible
im–, in–	in, into	import, income
inter–	between, among	interrupt, intercept, intercede
mid–	middle	midterm, midway
mis–	bad, wrong	misinterpret, misspell
non–	not, without	nonconformist, nonfiction, nonviolent
over–	excessive	overeat, overconfident
peri–	around, about	perimeter, periphery
pre–	before	preexisting, precedent, preview
re–, red–	again, back, against, behind	recede, redo, retreat, rewrite
semi–	half, partial	semiconscious, semicircle
sub–	under	subway, submarine
super–	above, beyond	superfluous, superhuman, superior
trans–	across, over, through, beyond	transmit, transgression, transit
un–	not, opposite of	unusual, unashamed, unfair

Suffixes

SUFFIXES are the same as prefixes except that suffixes are added to the ends of words rather than the beginnings.

Table 2.7 lists some common suffixes, their meanings, and examples.

Table 2.7. Common Suffixes

SUFFIX	MEANING	EXAMPLES
–able, –ible	is, can be	excitable, moveable, collectible
–al, –ial	having characteristics of, pertaining to	facial, procedural, universal
–cide, –cidum	kill	homicide, insecticide
–ed	past tense	arrested, called, treated
–en	made of, to cause to be	awaken, frighten, weaken
–er, –or	a person who	pioneer, professor, volunteer
–er	more	taller, meaner, shorter
–est	the most	fastest, meanest, shortest
–ful	full of	helpful, shameful, thankful
–ic	relating to, having characteristics of	poetic, dogmatic, organic
–ing	present participles, materials	sleeping, eating, bedding, frosting
–ion, –tion, –ation, –sion	act, process	submission, celebration, navigation
–ity, –cy –ty	state of, condition	activity, civility, normalcy, society
–ive, –ative, –itive	quality of	active, qualitative, sensitive
–ize	to make (forms a verb)	compartmentalize, mechanize
–less	without	blameless, homeless, remorseless
–ly	in the manner of	bravely, courageously, horrifically
–ment	state of being, act of	contentment, placement, resentment
–ness	state of, condition of	weakness, kindness
–ology	study	biology, physiology, sociology
–ous, –eous, –ious	having qualities of, full of	riotous, hazardous, righteous, gracious
–y	characterized by	sassy, cheeky, slimy

Examples

In the following questions, choose the word from the answer choices that is closest in meaning to the underlined word.

16. The suspect did not have any <u>OUTSTANDING</u> warrants.

    (A) inactive
    (B) unsettled
    (C) unconfirmed
    (D) confirmed

17. Because a career in law enforcement can be dangerous, officers should not become <u>COMPLACENT</u>.

   (A) confident
   (B) unsafe
   (C) self-satisfied
   (D) cheerful

18. During her testimony, the witness <u>RECANTED</u> her statement.

   (A) affirmed
   (B) rescinded
   (C) retold
   (D) regretted

19. The jury did not believe the suspect's mother was a <u>CREDIBLE</u> witness.

   (A) trustworthy
   (B) likeable
   (C) suitable
   (D) useful

20. The suspect's account of the incident was full of <u>DISCREPANCIES</u>.

   (A) falsities
   (B) inaccuracies
   (C) deception
   (D) inconsistencies

SPELLING

Why is spelling important in law enforcement? Much of what officers write is by hand, at least initially. What's more, any notes or other material an officer writes in connection with a crime or criminal investigation is *discoverable*. That means the court can compel an officer to turn over his or her notes and communications to the court and lawyers for both sides. Right or wrong, spelling could affect the officer's credibility and competence in the eyes of a jury. Many people believe multiple spelling and grammatical errors show a lack of attention to detail and a tendency toward sloppy work. Both are detrimental to effective police work.

Thankfully, spelling is the easiest part of the examination to study for. And while you could relegate yourself to simply repetitively writing random words on a piece of paper like you did after school when you were in trouble with the teacher, there are more focused methods to improve your performance on a multiple-choice spelling test. It can help to learn the following tips, tricks, and rules to prevent common spelling errors.

Homophones

HOMOPHONES are words that sound alike but are spelled differently and hold different meanings, such as *break* and *brake*.

Officer Brady stepped on the <u>brake</u> to stop the car.

Officer Brady took a lunch <u>break</u> during his shift.

Commonly confused words include:

- **ACCEPT**: agree
  EXCEPT: not including

- **ALOUD**: said out loud
  ALLOWED: able to

- **BARE**: uncovered
  BEAR: large animal; to carry

- **BRAKE**: to stop
  BREAK: to damage or interrupt

- **DIE**: to no longer be alive
  DYE: to artificially change color

- **EFFECT**: result (noun)
  AFFECT: to change (verb)

- **FLOUR**: used for cooking
  FLOWER: grows out of the ground

- **HEAL**: to get better
  HEEL: the back part of the foot

- **HOLE**: an opening
  WHOLE: all of something

- **INSURE**: to have insurance (*I need to insure my car.*)
  ENSURE: to make sure something happens (*She ensured that the dog found a good home.*)

- **MEAT**: the flesh of an animal
  MEET: to see someone

- **MORNING**: the start of the day
  MOURNING: grieving

- **PATIENCE**: tolerating annoyances
  PATIENTS: people receiving medical care

- **PEACE**: not at war
  PIECE: a part of something

- **POOR**: having very little money
  POUR: to dispense from a container

- **PRINCIPAL**: the leader or administrative head of a school
  PRINCIPLE: a strongly held belief

- **RAIN**: precipitation
  REIN: a strap that controls an animal
  REIGN: to rule over

- **RIGHT**: correct; a legal entitlement
  RITE: a ritual
  WRITE: to put words on paper

- **STAIR**: used to get from one floor to another
  STARE: a long, fixed look

- **SUITE**: a set of rooms
  SWEET: the taste associated with sugar

- **THEIR**: belonging to them (*they brought their luggage*)
  THERE: a place (*the luggage is over there*)
  THEY'RE: they are (*they're looking for the luggage*)

- **THROUGH**: to go in one side and out the other
  THREW: tossed (past tense of *throw*)

- **TO**: the preposition indicating movement or purpose (*I am going to work to do my job*)
  TOO: in addition (*I'm coming too*)
  TWO: more than one; dual (*two officers patrol this area together*)

- **WEAR**: to put on (*I'll wear my new dress.*)
  WHERE: to question about place (*Where is the door?*)

- **YOUR**: belonging to you (*your car*)
  YOU'RE: you are (*you're going to need a new car*)

Commonly Confused Words

Some words are similar in meaning, but not synonyms. However, they are commonly confused in writing and speech. A hallmark of good writing is the proper use of these words.

Table 2.8 contains some commonly confused words.

Table 2.8. Commonly Confused Words

CONFUSED WORDS	DEFINITION
Amount	describes a noncountable quantity (*an unknown amount of jewelry was stolen*)
Number	describes a countable quantity (*an unknown number of necklaces was stolen*)
Bring	toward the speaker (*bring to me*)
Take	away from the speaker (*take away from me*)
Farther	a measurable distance (*the house farther up the road*)
Further	more or greater (*explain further what you mean*)
Fewer	a smaller amount of something plural (*fewer chairs*)
Less	a smaller amount of something that cannot be counted (*less water*)
Lose	to fail to win; to not be able to find something (*to lose a game; to lose one's keys*)
Loose	relaxed; not firmly in place (*my pants are loose*)

Special Spelling Rules

i comes before *e* except after *c*

Generally, the letter *i* comes before the letter *e* in a word except when the *i* is preceded by the letter *c*.

- p<u>ie</u>ce
- sal<u>ie</u>nt
- c<u>ei</u>ling
- con<u>cei</u>vable

> Be cautious of the rule "*i* before *e* except after *c*," for it has many exceptions: "Your foreign neighbors weighed the iciest beige glaciers!"

There are some notable exceptions where the letter e comes before the letter i, such as:

- words that end in *–cient*, like *proficient* or *ancient*
- plural words ending in *–cies*, like *policies*
- words with an *ay* sound, like *eight*, *vein*, or *neighbor*

When adding a suffix to a word that ends in *y*, change the final *y* to an *i*.

- lazy → laziest
- tidy → tidily

For words that end with the letters *–le*, replace the letter *e* with the letter *y*: subtle → subtly

Plurals

Regular nouns are made plural by adding *s*. Irregular nouns can follow many different rules for pluralization, which are summarized in the table below.

Table 2.9. Irregular Plural Nouns

ENDS WITH . . .	MAKE IT PLURAL BY . . .	EXAMPLE
y	changing *y* to *i* and adding *–es*	baby → babies
f	changing *f* to *v* and adding *–es*	leaf → leaves
fe	changing *f* to *v* and adding *–s*	knife → knives
o	adding *–es*	potato → potatoes
us	changing *–us* to *–i*	nucleus → nuclei

ALWAYS THE SAME	DOESN'T FOLLOW THE RULES
sheep	man → men
deer	child → children
fish	person → people
moose	tooth → teeth
pants	goose → geese
binoculars	mouse → mice
scissors	ox → oxen

Pluralize words ending in *–ch*, *–s*, *–sh*, *–x*, or *–z* by adding *–es* to the end.

- catch → catches
- pass → passes
- push → pushes
- annex → annexes
- blitz → blitzes

An exception to the *–ch* rule includes words where the *ch* makes a *k* sound. For those words, simply add the letter *s* to the end of the word: stomach → stomachs.

Possessives Versus Contractions

A CONTRACTION is a combination of two words that is shortened by using an apostrophe to indicate the missing letter or letters. For instance, *cannot* is shortened to *can't*; the apostrophe stands in for the missing letters *n* and *o*.

A POSSESSIVE is a word with an apostrophe added to indicate possession. For example, rather than writing "the duty belt that belongs to Pat," write "Pat's duty belt."

A notable exception to this rule—and a common mistake—is the improper use of the contraction *it's* as a possessive, *its*.

The contraction for *it is* or *it has* is *it's*: "It's dangerous in that area of town at night."

The word *its* is possessive and shows ownership of the pronoun *it*, such as "the jury reached *its* verdict" or "the suspect's car was badly damaged, and *its* license plate was obscured."

Conjugating Verbs

The suffixes *–ed* or *–ing* added to a regular verb generally signify the verb's tense. For example, the present tense of the verb *to question* is *question* ("You question the suspect while I write the report.")

To show that the event happened in the past (or to form the past tense), the word *question* becomes *questioned*. And to refer to an action that is still happening (or to form the present participle), *question* becomes *questioning*. (See above for more details on conjugating verbs.)

There are some exceptions to the general rules for conjugating regular verbs.

For verbs ending with a silent *–e*, drop the *–e* before adding *–ed* or *–ing*.

- fake → faked → faking
- ache → ached → aching

When verbs end in the letters *–ee*, do not drop the second *e*. Instead, simply add *–d* or *–ing*.

- free → freed → freeing
- agree → agreed → agreeing

When the verb ends with a single vowel plus a consonant, and the stress is at the end of the word, then the consonant must be doubled before adding *–ed* or *–ing*.

- commit → committed → committing
- refer → referred → referring

If the stress is not at the end of the word, then the consonant can remain singular.

- target → targeted → targeting
- visit → visited → visiting

Verbs that end with the letter *c* must have the letter *k* added before receiving a suffix: panic → panicked → panicking

Examples

Read the following sentences and choose the correct spelling of the missing word.

21. The defendant asked the court to show him _____ in the punishment for his crime.

(A) lienency

(B) leniency

(C) leneincy

(D) leanency

22. Deputy Smith found _____ in the inmate's cell.

(A) contriband

(B) controband

(C) contraband

(D) contreband

23. Evidence that is fleeting or that can fade away over time is said to be of an _____ nature.

(A) effervescent

(B) evanecent

(C) evanescent

(D) evenescent

24. Officer Jones attempted to _____ the victim's blood loss by applying pressure to the wound.

(A) mitagate

(B) mitegate

(C) midigate

(D) mitigate

ANSWER KEY

1. (C) Correct. *Minnesota* and *August* are proper nouns, and *coat* and *gloves* are common nouns. *I* is a pronoun, and *warm* is an adjective that modifies coat.

2. (A) Correct. *New* modifies the noun *chef*, and *boiling* modifies the noun *soup*.

   (B) Incorrect. *Carefully* is an adverb modifying the verb *stirred*.

   (C) Incorrect. *Heat* is a noun.

   (D) Incorrect. *Lowered* is a verb.

3. (A) Incorrect. *To* frequently indicates position; it does not make sense here.

   (B) Incorrect. *With* often implies a physical connection; it does not make sense here.

   (C) Correct. The correct preposition is *of*. The preposition *of* usually shows a relationship and may accompany a verb.

   (D) Incorrect. *About* is not idiomatically paired with *love* and is thus incorrect.

4. (A) Correct. Choice A should use quotation marks to set off a direct quote: *"I love apple pie!" John exclaimed with a smile.*

5. (B) Correct. The sentence is a question, so it should end with a question mark.

6. (A) Correct. The phrase is a prepositional phrase beginning with the preposition *with*. The preposition *with* modifies *the eager students*.

7. (A) Correct. In this sentence, the conjunction is joining together two contrasting ideas, so the correct answer is *but*.

8. (A) Incorrect. In this sentence, *hats* and *shoes* and *them* are all plural; they agree.

   (B) Correct. *The members of the band* is plural (*members*), so it should be replaced by the plural pronoun *their* instead of the singular *her*.

   (C) Incorrect. *Janitor* is singular, so the singular pronouns *his or her* are correct.

   (D) Incorrect. *You* and *you* agree in person and number. Note here that the pronoun *them* agrees with the antecedent *someone*. This is generally accepted usage, but it is unlikely to appear on an exam.

9. (B) Correct. Choice A contains a vague reference; it is unclear who was shot.

10. (B) Correct. This sentence contains a verb error; the verb is should be plural: are. All plural indefinite pronouns agree with plural verbs. Here, the subject of the sentence, *some*, is a plural indefinite pronoun, so it requires a plural verb.

11. (A) Correct. The phrase *by this time tomorrow* describes an action that will take place and be completed in the future, so the future perfect tense (*will have arrived*) should be used.

12. **(D)** **Correct.** This sentence should read, "Of the four speeches, Jerry's was the longest." The word *long* has only one syllable, so it should be modified with the suffix *–est*, not the word *most*.

13. **(A)** **Correct.** Choice B has a misplaced modifier (the word *often*).

14. **(A)** **Correct.** Choice B contains a sentence fragment.

15. **(B)** **Correct.** Choice A is a run-on sentence.

16. (A)   Incorrect. *Inactive* means *dormant*.

    (B)   **Correct.** *Unsettled* means *outstanding* or *due*.

    (C)   Incorrect. *Unconfirmed* means *unsupported* or *uncorroborated*.

    (D)   Incorrect. *Confirmed* means *verified*.

17. (A)   Incorrect. *Confident* means *sure* or *secure*.

    (B)   Incorrect. *Unsafe* means *dangerous* or *risky*.

    (C)   **Correct.** *Self-satisfied* means *complacent*.

    (D)   Incorrect. *Cheerful* means *pleasant* or *happy*.

18. (A)   Incorrect. *Affirmed* means *to maintain as true* or *confirm*.

    (B)   **Correct.** *Rescinded* means *recant*.

    (C)   Incorrect. *Retold* means *told over again in a new way*.

    (D)   Incorrect. *Regretted* means *felt remorse for*.

19. **(A)**   **Correct.** *Trustworthy* means *credible*.

    (B)   Incorrect. *Likeable* means *easy to like*.

    (C)   Incorrect. *Suitable* means *appropriate*.

    (D)   Incorrect. *Useful* means *being of use*.

20. (A)   Incorrect. *Falsities* means *lies*.

    (B)   Incorrect. *Inaccuracies* means *errors* or *mistakes*.

    (C)   Incorrect. *Deception* means *ruse* or *trick*.

    (D)   **Correct.** *Inconsistencies* means *discrepancies*.

21. **(B)**   **Correct.** *Leniency* is the correct spelling.

22. **(C)**   **Correct.** *Contraband* is the correct spelling.

23. **(C)**   **Correct.** *Evanescent* is the correct spelling.

24. **(D)**   **Correct.** *Mitigate* is the correct spelling.

3

REASONING, SPATIAL ORIENTATION, AND MEMORIZATION

On the CJBAT, you will see questions on inductive reasoning, deductive reasoning, information ordering, and problem sensitivity.

You will also be tested on your skills in visual analysis and attention to detail. These are the spatial orientation and memorization questions. These questions are discussed at the end of this chapter.

WHAT IS REASONING?

REASONING is the ability to apply logical skills and cognitive aptitudes to the FACTS (i.e., the indisputable evidence or crucial pieces of information) of a situation in order to make a sound decision. Officers use LOGIC to assess and organize the facts or evidence of a particular scenario or situation. Reasoning is tested in the field of criminal justice because police officers, state troopers, and correctional officers work under life-and-death circumstances that demand they acutely understand complex relationships and convey a clear understanding of the most important facts.

INDUCTIVE REASONING

What is Inductive Reasoning?

Within the context of law enforcement or corrections, inductive reasoning is the ability to analyze the facts in order to hypothesize whether a particular rule, trend, or concept fits the situation or scenario. This analytical skill comes in handy when trying to understand the events or sequence of a particular crime or trying to trace/map a series of related crimes. It also comes in handy when analyzing any kind of chart, graph, or data.

How is Inductive Reasoning Tested in Law Enforcement?

On the CJBAT, test takers must draw conclusions about quantitative information provided in the form of charts, graphs, or data sets. They must deduce which rules, trends, or concepts fit the quantitative information offered.

CHARTS are data visualization tools that outline or exhibit certain data sets or categories, usually in tabular form. TABLES, which might look like an Excel spreadsheet, list key facts and compare these facts across categories via rows and columns. The top row, as illustrated in the table in Figure 3.1, is usually the *title row* with all the titles of each column. The first column usually dictates the main category (in Figure 3.1, "Year/degree of injury") that will be compared across the other column categories. The other column categories in this table include "Fatal," Serious," "Slight," and "Total." In this particular table, there are computations offered in the last column ("Total") and the last row ("Percent increase"). All rows offer the concrete numerical data that ties the dates of the first column with the categories of the top row.

YEAR/DEGREE OF INJURY	FATAL	SERIOUS	SLIGHT	TOTAL
1998 – 1999	49	162	653	**864**
1999 – 2000	62	200	933	**1195**
2000 – 2001	72	244	1066	**1382**
2001 – 2002	95	392	1390	**1877**
2002 – 2003	80	416	1683	**2179**
2003 – 2004	68	437	1862	**2367**
2004 – 2005	77	411	3424	**3912**
2005 – 2006	49	476	3296	**3821**
2006 – 2007	58	-	-	-
Percent increase 98/99–05/06 or 06/07	18	194	405	**342**

Figure 3.1. Table

A GRAPH is a data visualization diagram that represents that variation of a variable in comparison to one or more differing variables. All graphs have labels.

- The MAIN TITLE offers a brief explanation of what is in the graph. Titles help the audience to understand the "main point" or "main claim" of a graph.

- The SUBTITLE offers more specific information about the purpose of the graph. Subtitles are brief sentences or phrases that enhance main titles.

- Bar graphs and line graphs have an *X*-AXIS; the *x*-axis runs horizontally (flat). The *x*-axis has quantities representing different categories, statistics, or times that are being compared.

- Bar graphs and line graphs have a *Y*-AXIS; the *y*-axis runs vertically (up and down). The *y*-axis usually measures quantities, typically starting at 0 or another designated number.

The two generic graphs in Figures 3.2 and 3.3—a bar graph and a line graph—illustrate where labels are located. In some cases, the subtitle can be placed below or beside the main title.

Both types of graphs—bar graphs and line graphs—show *trends*, or prevailing developments, tendencies, or inclinations that can be extrapolated from the graph. The trends of the BAR GRAPH in Figure 3.2 compare two categories: male versus female (in terms of the broader category of victims of violent crime). LINE GRAPHS, on the other hand, usually show change over time. The trend that emerges in the bar graph is that, from 2013 to 2016, women were more likely to be the victims of violent crime. One trend that emerges in the line graph is that burglary declined from 2004 to 2008.

Figure 3.2. Bar Graph

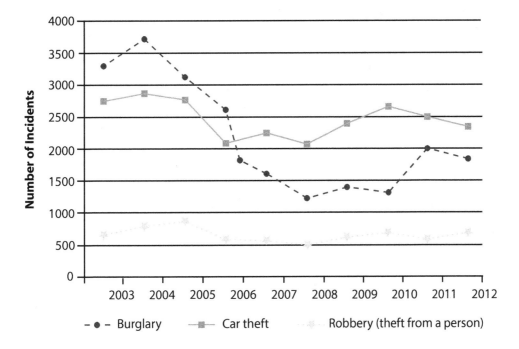

Figure 3.3. Line Graph

Examples

Use the graph to answer the questions below.

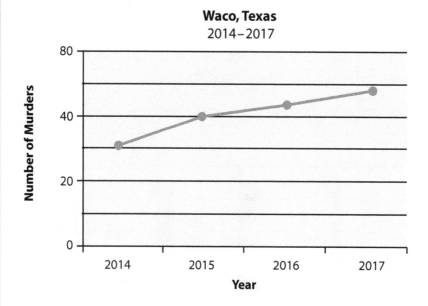

Waco, Texas
2014–2017

1. According to the graph above, what can be concluded about the murder rate in Waco, Texas?

   A) It has declined from 2014 – 2017.

   B) It has increased from 2014 – 2017.

   C) It remained the same from 2014 – 2017.

   D) It increased in 2014 – 2016, but it decreased in 2017.

2. A program was recently instituted to fight against the rising murder rate in Waco, Texas. However, the program only lasted one year due to budget cuts. What year was this program most likely cut?

   A) 2014

   B) 2015

   C) 2016

   D) 2017

DEDUCTIVE REASONING

What is Deductive Reasoning?

Within the context of law enforcement or corrections, deductive reasoning is employed when a member of a department or agency is able to apply protocols and procedures to specific situations or use knowledge of these protocols and procedures to come to logical conclusions. One example of deductive reasoning is deciding whether to arrest an alleged perpetrator of a domestic incident based on the rules and regulations (i.e., the step-by-step details) provided by the department or agency. Deductive reasoning is useful in law enforcement or corrections because officers and agents are continually placed into situations where they must be able to apply the rules in order to reach a conclusion.

How is Deductive Reasoning Tested in Law Enforcement?

On the CJBAT, future police officers and correctional officers must read passages that explain state or local policies, most likely Florida state law. In order to demonstrate their deductive reasoning skills, they also have to read specific scenarios and decide the best course of action for approaching these scenarios based on the policies they just read.

Examples

Below is an example of a general domestic incident response order that may be used in a police department:

I. POLICY

Domestic violence is a serious crime, one that affects both the individual and society. Our department seeks to reduce all incidents of domestic violence through coordinated partnerships with law enforcement agencies, victims, and communities. Recognizing that domestic violence escalates in its severity and frequency over time, our department advocates for early intervention, especially in households that have already been documented "at risk." Officers will treat these incidents in the same professional manner as all other law enforcement requests, providing immediate and effective assistance. Recognizing our state's Domestic Violence Act (DVA), we plan to protect victims from these devastating incidents, using all reasonable means necessary to prevent further abuse. These reasonable means may include the arrest of an alleged offender if there is probable cause.

II. INITIAL RESPONSE

I. Whenever a law enforcement officer responds to a domestic incident, he or she must immediately use all reasonable means to prevent further abuse, neglect, or exploitation. These means include the potential need to

1. restore order by asserting control of the situation.
2. identify and secure any weapons or objects that can be used as weapons.
3. determine if medical assistance is needed.
   a. If medical assistance is needed, the law enforcement officer must call for an ambulance or arrange for the victim's transfer to a hospital.
   b. If the victim refuses treatment, the law enforcement officer must advise the victim of the importance of getting medical attention.

II. If another department member is involved in the domestic incident, the responding member must request that a department member of higher rank be present.

Answer the following questions using the information from the text.

3. An officer arrives on scene at a domestic incident at 345 N. Landover Street. When the officer arrives at the residence, she realizes that the alleged perpetrator happens to be one of her fellow officers at the Landover Precinct. The fellow officer is wielding a weapon at his wife, who appears to be seriously injured. What is the proper sequence for responding to this situation, keeping in mind the general orders regarding domestic violence for the department?

A) restore order by securing the weapon and the neutralizing the aggressor, call for an ambulance, notify a higher-ranking officer

B) notify a higher-ranking officer, wait for the higher-ranking officer to arrive, and call for an ambulance

C) call for an ambulance, notify a higher-ranking officer, and restore order by securing the weapon and the neutralizing the aggressor

D) restore order by securing the weapon and the neutralizing the aggressor, call for an ambulance, and file the necessary paperwork

4. What happens if the victim refuses medical attention?

A) take her into the precinct for private questioning

B) respect her rights as a victim and simply document it in your paperwork

C) advise the victim of the importance of getting medical attention

D) report the incident to a higher-ranking police officer

PROBLEM SENSITIVITY

PROBLEM SENSITIVITY is the ability to use common sense to recognize that something is wrong or is likely to go wrong. Common sense is the ability to use common or basic facts (e.g., body language, evidence, or statements) to remain sensitive that there is or may be a problem. It is the ability to recognize that there is a problem embedded within a particular moment or situation. Police officers and correctional officers are expected to be sensitive to the *whole problem* as well as *the underlying components of that problem*. Using the ongoing example of domestic incidents, problem sensitivity would manifest itself in a law enforcement officer's ability to use signs (e.g., body language, evidence, or statements) to recognize that an underlying conflict might be in progress between family members.

On the CJBAT, problem sensitivity questions typically take form as a short passage that the test taker must read in order to extrapolate any major issues or problems. In some cases, the test taker may be asked to explain the conditions or root causes of the problem.

Identifying, Not Solving, Problems

PROBLEM SENSITIVITY is not about being solution oriented. It is about paying extreme attention to detail, or having the ability to focus on specific components of a passage—in this case, to identify the problem or its root causes/conditions. It is also the ability to draw conclusions, or logically "pull information" (i.e., key words, facts, and sentences), from a text in order to make a claim. In this context, the claim is identifying the problem or its root causes/conditions.

You are not being tested on solving the problem. Rather, the exam is testing candidates on their ability to identify the problem and/or its root causes or conditions. The problem sensitivity portion of the exam is about paying attention to details and drawing conclusions that identify the problem(s) embedded in these details.

Below are examples of problem sensitivity questions you might see on the CJBAT.

Examples

Officers Morales and Davidson were called to the scene of an apparent physical altercation between a father and his eight-year-old son. The child had previously called 9-1-1, claiming that his father had punched him in the throat. Officer Morales approached the family to see if everything was all right. The child, now holding his father's hand, tells the officers in a wheezing voice that he was just lying because he was upset that his father took away his video games. He apologizes to the officers, claiming "all of this was my fault, I swear." Officer Davidson notices evident bruising along the child's neck as well as the apparent wheezing in his voice. Officer Morales also notices the father gripping the child's hand tightly. Officer Davidson asks the child why he has bruises and why he is wheezing. The boy anxiously replies that he had slipped and fell while he was throwing a fit over his video game. Both officers are suspicious of this story.

5. After analyzing this scenario, what important details can be extracted to use as evidence of a potential problem?

   A) the boy's statement that it was his fault

   B) the fact that the father and son were holding hands

   C) the boy's claim that it was about a dispute over video games

   D) the evident wheezing and bruising

Officer Bridges is patrolling a city park around 2:15 a.m. when he notices a car speeding through a stop sign on the closest street. He pulls the car over for a routine traffic stop. As he walks over to the vehicle, he notices the driver snap back quickly into a normal sitting position after fiddling around in the glove compartment. The driver remains stiff in posture, rapidly claiming, "I know I rolled that stop sign officer, but I am just a little tired." The driver says it "won't happen again" and asks for forgiveness just this one time. There are no signs of alcohol or drug use. The driver is cognizant but anxious. Officer Bridges asks the driver, "What were you doing in your glove compartment?" The driver snaps back: "What is it with you cops always being up in my business? Can't you just let me go? I just rolled a stop sign." The driver apologizes for "losing his cool," but ignores the initial question. When asked the question again, he ignores it and focuses back on the apology. A third attempt at the question has the same result for Officer Bridges.

6. Based on the details provided about the situation, what is likely the problem?

   A) The driver is just impatient and has little faith in police officers.

   B) The driver is intoxicated.

   C) The driver is concealing something in his glove compartment.

   D) The driver is hiding drugs in his glove compartment.

SPATIAL ORIENTATION

What is Spatial Orientation?

SPATIAL ORIENTATION questions attempt to assess the visualization ability of law enforcement officers. In particular, spatial orientation questions evaluate law enforcement or correctional officers' ability to understand their relation to a particular object, location, or set of objects or locations. On the CJBAT, test takers receive a map (with a key and compass). The map is accompanied by a scenario. Typically, test takers have to use the map and the scenario to determine the shortest distance between locations or objects on the map. Likewise, spatial orientation questions may also quiz aspiring officers on the relationship(s) between objects and locations.

Spatial Orientation in Law Enforcement

Spatial orientation requires both memorization (of place) and directional orientation. These skills are important for officers because they allow them to stay oriented once directions or locations are changed. Officers must be able to find quick routes to and from emergencies, and they must be able to change directions to effectively respond to crimes and/or crises.

Examples

7. Officers Dalton and Mills have parked their police cruiser at the intersection of 2nd Avenue and the train tracks. They receive a call to respond to a violent assault at the southwestern corner of Pine Park. What is the only route they can take in their police cruiser to make it to the site of the incident?

A) travel south on 2nd Avenue, west on Oak Boulevard, and north on Main Street

B) travel north on 2nd Avenue, west on Oak Boulevard, and south on Main Street

C) travel north on 2nd Avenue, east on Oak Boulevard, and north on Main Street

D) travel north on 2nd Avenue, east on Oak Boulevard, and south on Main Street

8. A call from a concerned citizen at the Sycamore Apartments reported that she had witnessed a burglary from her window. The person claimed the burglary took place right on the street near Pine Park. Based on the map, the witness's window was likely facing

   A) north.

   B) south.

   C) east.

   D) west.

INFORMATION ORDERING

INFORMATION ORDERING is the power to apply the proper instructions, rules, or orders to a particular situation or scenario while maintaining an appropriate sequence. Information ordering assesses a candidate's ability to understand and apply procedures. This is important in law enforcement because many protocols, orders, and laws are sequential and procedural.

Example

Officer Lopez just finished responding to a domestic incident at 225 Main Street. The following seven statements appeared in the victim's recorded testimony:

1. I ran upstairs to the bedroom to get away from the incident.

2. I locked the bedroom door behind me to prevent him from hitting me.

3. My husband got mad at me because I was denying the incident.

4. My husband claimed that I cheated on him with a neighbor.

5. I told him I was not a woman who would cheat on her husband.

6. He became so angry that he punched me in my jaw.

7. He kicked down the bedroom door, and that is when I called the police.

9. What is the most logical ordering of these statements?

   A) 1, 2, 3, 4, 5, 6, 7

   B) 2, 4, 3, 1, 6, 5, 7

   C) 4, 5, 3, 6, 1, 2, 7

   D) 1, 7, 4, 5, 3, 6, 2

MEMORIZATION

MEMORIZATION is the ability to recall specific evidence, facts, or details about a certain policy, event, or incident. Memorization is a key skill for law enforcement and correctional officers because while on active duty, all officers need to observe and remember the details of an event or its contexts, and they need to be alert at every scene. Memorization is the foundation of observation and alertness in the field.

Observation and alertness allow officers to not only respond appropriately to dangerous situations, but also *recall* those situations for documentation, criminalization, and legal cases. Observation and alertness protect officers both on and off duty.

On criminal justice certification examinations, memorization questions usually follow the exhibition of a particular photograph (which is viewed for a limited amount of time). Aspiring officers have to recall what they witnessed in the photograph.

Examples

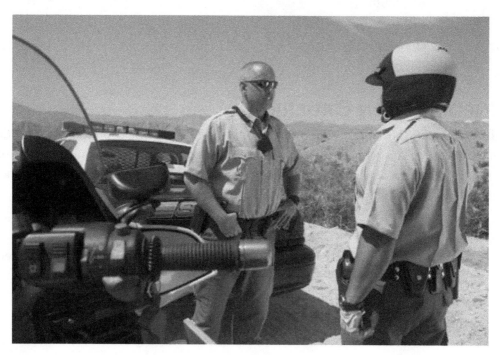

10. How many officers are depicted in the photograph?
    A) 1
    B) 2
    C) 3
    D) 4

11. Where was the picture most likely taken?
    A) by the railroad tracks
    B) at the police station
    C) on the side of the road
    D) in a parking lot

1. **B)** **Correct.** The line graph shows a gradual increase from 2014 to 2017, which is indicated by the upward slant of the line and the difference in data from 2014 to 2017. The number of murders in 2014, indicated by the first dot of the line graph from left to right, was roughly thirty. The number of murders in 2017 was closer to sixty. The movement from a lower number to a higher number shows an increase.

2. **C)** **Correct.** The murder rate plateaus, or flattens, from 2015 to 2016. This was likely the year that the program to fight against the murder rate was instituted. The increase in the rate from 2016 to 2017 logically indicates that that was likely the year the program was disbanded.

3. **A)** **Correct.** This choice follows the response orders recommended in the policy above: (1) "restore order by asserting control of the situation," (2) "identify and secure any weapons or objects that can be used as weapons," and (3a) "if medical assistance is needed, the law enforcement officer must call for an ambulance or arrange for the victim's transfer to a hospital." It also respects policy recommendation II.II: "If another department member is involved in the domestic incident, the responding member must request a department member of higher rank."

4. **C)** **Correct.** According to policy II.I.3.a, "If the victim refuses treatment, the law enforcement officer must advise the victim of the importance of getting medical attention."

5. **D)** **Correct.** The "wheezing and bruising," especially when viewed through the perspective of the original call of a physical altercation, are documentable details that indicate a domestic violence case may have occurred. The boy's apology and claims about the video game might be untrue. The father holding the son's hand might be a sign of control, not comfort. The wheezing and bruising, however, are evidence of a possible injury.

6. **C)** **Correct.** The driver is specifically avoiding addressing the officer's question about his glove compartment. All the other answer choices simply address assumptions instead of details or facts. The facts state that the driver was fiddling around in his glove compartment, he is irritable and agitated, and he is ignoring questions. It is logical that he might be concealing something in the glove compartment. He may be impatient or dislike police officers, but that conclusion ignores the driver's failure to address the officer's questions about the glove compartment. Claiming the driver is intoxicated or hiding drugs is only an assumption because there is no evidence of alcohol or drugs; the officer does not smell alcohol or marijuana, nor does he observe drug paraphernalia.

7. **B)** **Correct.** There is no southbound, eastbound, or westbound road at this intersection. The only place to go is north toward Oak Boulevard. Since north

is the only logical first move by car, the cruiser has to then move west on Oak Boulevard, past City Hall, and south on Main Street, past the train station.

8. **C)** **Correct.** Pine Park is due east of Sycamore Apartments, according to the map. Thus, it is likely that the window was facing in that direction. If it were facing in any other direction, Pine Park would not be visible.

9. **C)** **Correct.** Causally and logically speaking, in reverse order, the bedroom door would have to be closed or locked (number 2) before it is kicked down (number 7), ruling out choice D. They would have to relocate upstairs first in order to even be in that space (number 1). There would have to be a reason to lock the door and run upstairs (number 6). The violent act would likely be rooted in anger (number 3). The anger would likely be rooted in an action/conflict/disagreement/statement (numbers 5 and 4). But the only logical causality of that conflict, at least in this case, is that there was an original claim (number 4) followed by a counterclaim (number 5).

10. **B)** **Correct.** There are two officers in the photo.

11. **C)** **Correct.** The officers are likely standing by the side of the road; a cruiser and motorcycle are pulled over, and they are standing by brush overlooking mountains.

4

PRACTICE TEST

WRITTEN COMPREHENSION

Read the passage carefully, and then answer the following questions.

Passage One

(1)

When people think critically, they examine, evaluate, and synthesize information they have gathered in order to arrive at a logical conclusion. Critical thinking can be accomplished at a simple or more probing level, depending on whether a cursory or more thoughtful conclusion is desired. At its most basic level, critical thinking is an activity necessary for people to function properly in society. Every day, without thought, most people engage in simple critical thinking exercises as they interact with one another. They observe, analyze, and assess clues and information around them in order to understand others' behavior and to make decisions about how to respond appropriately. When used purposefully, critical thinking can help one gain a much greater understanding of the gathered information. However, many people do not wish to move beyond this basic, instinctual level when deep critical thinking is not **IMPERATIVE**. They do not wish to gain deeper understanding of a person or issue even though gaining such understanding may be as simple as asking, "Why?"

(2)

Intensive critical thinking is employed most often in academic settings. Teachers challenge students to apply a higher order of thinking skills to avoid oversimplification, to be objective, and to always ask the next question such as "Why?" "What?" or "What if?" to make reasoned judgments. Critical thinking in academia generally requires a supposition, facts and information, and the ability to infer a logical conclusion from one or more assertions. In academia, critical thinking can either be relegated to mere theoretical dialogue or be applied to an actual problem in order to generate improved conditions.

(3)

Since the 1970s, critical thinking has also been used in police work. It is vital, purposeful, and systematic. Police must analyze crimes and criminal activity, establish facts, and determine what information remains unknown. Police investigators analyze patterns and evidence to determine how and why criminal activity was committed and who committed the crime. They ask the questions "What's missing?" "What are the benefits of the crime?" "Who benefited?" "Was the crime planned or opportunistic?" Each question probes deeper into the issue and helps investigators uncover clues to reconstruct other people's reasoning. Critical thinking in police work questions the known facts of a case in such a way that investigators are able to understand criminal actions, and those who commit them, more accurately. Such thinking can help investigators understand a perpetrator's state of mind, determine what the perpetrator was thinking, how he or she was thinking, as well as establish the investigator's opinion of what, how, and why a particular event occurred.

(4)

Recently, critical thinking has become even more vital to law enforcement because criminals continue to become more **SAVVY**. As technology has evolved, so has crime sophistication. Criminals have to work smarter to avoid being apprehended, thus detectives work smarter by studying, evaluating, and assessing evidence to successfully investigate and prosecute criminals.

1. The tone of the author can be best described as:

   A) objective

   B) argumentative

   C) passionate

   D) empathetic

2. As used in paragraph 1, what is the best synonym for *imperative*:

   A) absolutely necessary

   B) very important

   C) of personal interest

   D) avoidable

3. According to the passage, it can be inferred that the author believes which of the following:

   I. Critical thinking is used in many ways.

   II. Critical thinking is only important in academia.

   III. Critical thinking is vital in police work.

   A) III only

   B) II only

   C) II and III only

   D) I and III only

4. Which of the following, if true, WEAKENS the main point of paragraph 3?

   A) People do not use critical thinking in everyday life.

   B) Law enforcement began using critical thinking methods in the 1990s.

   C) Academics do not apply theory to real-life situations.

   D) Critical thinking has reduced successful investigations and prosecutions of crimes.

5. As used in paragraph 4, what is the best definition of *savvy*?

   A) cool

   B) shrewd

   C) inexperienced

   D) dangerous

6. What is the best title for this passage?

   A) The Definition of Critical Thinking

   B) Critical Thinking and Law Enforcement

   C) The Many Applications of Critical Thinking

   D) Critical Thinking: A Survey

7. According to the passage, what is the main reason for the application of critical thinking in police work?

   A) to help investigators understand criminal activity and criminal perpetrators more accurately

   B) to determine how criminal activity was committed and who committed the crime

   C) because crime sophistication has evolved, and thus investigators must also evolve

   D) all of the above

Passage Two

River City Police Department policy mandates that officers remain in good physical condition while employed with the department. Most officers would gladly comply, but commute times, long work hours, and mandatory overtime account for about fifteen hours of each officer's day. Officers recently asked River City about developing a wellness program for staff members, sworn staff in particular, including the ability to exercise in one of the many gyms located at various River City Police Department's satellite facilities. The resulting memo from the River City chief of police was disseminated to all staff.

Dear Staff,

It gives me great pleasure to work at an agency that is full of hardworking, motivated individuals, sworn and civilians alike, who seek new ways to continue improving themselves in both professional and personal life.

As you are aware, law enforcement is a physical job that requires the men and women who do the job to maintain a high level of physical fitness. I'm confident all of you would like to maintain that high level of physical fitness. I know this is difficult for many who have family obligations and long commutes from your respective homes in the outlying areas, and for those who work copious overtime shifts. These factors have undoubtedly created barriers for you to reach your personal goals and the required baseline goals of this department.

It was recently brought to my attention that a number of you requested permission to exercise at your duty station during your workday, on your meal break, in one of the various gyms we maintain on facility sites, in order to make exercising easier to fit into your daily routine. I understand your various dilemmas, but for reasons of liability, workers' compensation issues, as well as the logistical issues involved in managing meal breaks so an entire duty station is not working out at the same time, I must deny that request. I will, however, work with you in other ways to help you meet your fitness goals.

As of next week, the following policies will take effect under the River City Police Employee Wellness Pledge program:

- We will update our meal program for staff members assigned to duty stations where leaving base during shifts is disallowed. We will no longer provide hamburgers, soda, french fries, bacon, or chips. For those of you who work the night shift and eat breakfast, eggs and hash brown potatoes will still be available. If you would like to purchase a soda or snack during your twelve-hour shift, you may do so at the remaining vending machines on-site.
- You may not exercise at any gym during duty hours, even if you are on break. You are welcome to work out before or after your assigned shift at any of our gyms.
- We will begin a physical fitness club that will meet once a month at one of our facilities for organized workouts. This club is open to the first 30 people who sign up. I, as well as the **WARRIORS** who already work out with me, would love for you to join us at our morning gym sessions.

Thank you for your diligence to do the job well and to make River City the best police department in the state. I look forward to helping you meet your fitness goals and to your feedback on this exciting new program.

Keep up the good work!

Sincerely,

Chief Jeff Hyde

8. What is the main point of the chief's letter?

   A) Physical fitness is important for police work.

   B) The chief is willing to help officers and staff stay fit.

   C) The chief does not want to be responsible for staff who exercise on duty.

   D) It is primarily the responsibility of the employee to manage time for workouts.

9. What is the overall tone of the chief's letter?

   A) cordial

   B) angry

   C) passionate

   D) overbearing

10. What is the best meaning of the word *warriors* as used in the passage?

    A) a person experienced in warfare

    B) a person who shows great vigor

    C) a person skilled in using weapons

    D) a person with fitness experience

11. According to the chief, what is the main reason he denied the request to work out during work hours?

    A) Staff should be working, not exercising.

    B) Even though staff may be on break, River City is still liable for injuries.

    C) It is difficult logistically to ensure not all staff are working out at the same time.

    D) Both B and C are correct.

12. According to the passage, how many hours in a given day does the average River City officer have left to eat, sleep, run errands, and work out after he or she released from duty?

    A) fifteen

    B) seventeen

    C) nine

    D) eleven

Passage Three

These days, it is harder than ever for kids to simply "walk away" from a bully. Bullying among children and adolescents has evolved beyond taunting a smaller or less popular kid while he or she is at school to cyberstalking children across city and state lines with the use of common electronic devices. Because of the increasing reach of bullies, among other things, suicides and violent confrontations among youth have risen over the years.

Because of the current scope of bullying, school administrators no longer rely solely on teachers to keep kids safe while at school. Rather, administrators build teams of collaborators that include health care workers, teachers, administration, security staff, and law enforcement personnel to ensure schools remain a safe place for kids to learn. School resource officers (SROs) receive training in issues that are unique to youth. Generally, SROs have an office on campus. They are stationed at the school and spend their time dealing with law enforcement issues. They also spend a great deal of time talking to kids about anything that interests them, such as school activities, sports, law enforcement, and life in general. Since SROs talk to kids at particular schools regularly, officers are in a unique position to identify emerging issues and prevent them before they develop into greater problems.

SROs play a large role in managing situations that involve bullying so that *all* involved students and families are heard and respected.

13. Which fact, if true, strengthens the author's main point?

    A) More kids are bullied currently than in previous years.

    B) The majority of bullying happens on school grounds.

    C) Funding for school resource officers has been reduced.

    D) Youth suicides are on the decline.

14. According to the passage, why are SROs important for managing bullying?

    A) SROs arrest students who are too aggressive.

    B) SROs get to know students and can prevent problems.

    C) SROs provide defensive training for victims of bullies.

    D) SROs help teachers learn to identify bullies.

15. According to the passage, why has bullying become so prevalent?

    A) increased negative behavior

    B) school resource officers on school grounds

    C) technological advancement

    D) boredom among children

WRITTEN EXPRESSION

1. Choose the word or phrase that correctly completes the sentence.

Because of its distance from the sun, the planet Neptune _____ that last the equivalent of forty-one Earth years.

A) have seasons

B) has seasons

C) have season

D) has season

2. Which of the following sentences does NOT contain an error?

A) The Iris and B. Gerald Cantor Roof Garden, atop the Metropolitan Museum of Art in New York City, offer a remarkable view.

B) The Mammoth-Flint Ridge Cave System, located in central Kentucky inside Mammoth Cave National Park, are the largest cave system in the world.

C) Andy Warhol's paintings, in addition to being the subject of the largest single-artist museum in the United States, are in great demand.

D) The field of child development are concerned with the emotional, psychological, and biological developments of infants and children.

3. Which of the following phrases contains an error in capitalization?

The *Chicago Tribune* is famous for many reasons: in 1948, the paper published an erroneous headline about the winner of the Presidential election, and in 1974, it called for President Nixon's resignation.

A) *Chicago Tribune*

B) the paper

C) about the winner

D) Presidential election

4. Which of the following punctuation marks is used incorrectly?

Ms. McIlvaine told her students that, although the Nile River, passes through eleven countries, it is the main water source of only two of them—Egypt and Sudan.

A) the comma after *that*

B) the comma after *River*

C) the comma after *countries*

D) the dash after *them*

5. Which sentence does NOT contain an error?

A) The grandchildren and their cousins enjoyed their day at the beach.

B) Most of the grass has lost their deep color.

C) The jury was cheering as their commitment comes to a close.

D) Every boy and girl must learns to behave themselves in school.

6. Which of the following punctuation marks is used incorrectly?

Our professor says that, though the term *nomad* is often associated with early populations, nomadic cultures exist today, especially in the mountain's of Europe and Asia.

A) the comma after *that*

B) the comma after *populations*

C) the comma after *today*

D) the apostrophe in *mountain's*

7. Choose the word or phrase that correctly completes the sentence.

Engineers _____ seat belts to stop the inertia of traveling bodies by applying an opposing force on the driver and passengers during a collision.

A) designing

B) design

C) was designing

D) will have designed

8. Choose the word or phrase that most correctly completes the sentence.

The employer decided that he could not, due to the high cost of health care, afford to offer _____ benefits to his employees.

A) for other

B) some other

C) no other

D) any other

9. Choose the word or phrase that correctly completes the sentence.

Though organized firefighting groups existed as early as Ancient Egypt, the first fully state-run brigade was created by Emperor Augustus of Rome _____ as the nation's official police force.

A) which also functioned

B) and also functioned

C) for also functioning

D) that also functioned

10. Which of the following sentences does NOT have an error?

A) In addition to the disastrous effects an active volcano can have on it's immediate surroundings, an eruption can also pose a threat to passing aircraft.

B) In addition to the disastrous effects an active volcano can have on it's immediate surroundings: an eruption can also pose a threat to passing aircraft.

C) In addition to the disastrous effects an active volcano can have on its immediate surroundings: an eruption can also pose a threat to passing aircraft!

D) In addition to the disastrous effects an active volcano can have on its immediate surroundings, an eruption can also pose a threat to passing aircraft.

Spelling

In the next five questions, choose the misspelled word. Only one word is misspelled in each sentence.

11. Pursuant to federal and state laws, all jails and prisons make reasonable accommadations for inmates who have disabilities to ensure they have the same or comparable access as inmates who do not have disabilities.

A) Pursuant

B) federal

C) accommadations

D) comparable

12. River City Police Department found itself under seige after an officer, who was chasing a dangerous criminal, crashed his patrol car into a storefront during business hours.

A) seige

B) dangerous

C) storefront

D) business

13. Sasha filed a restraining order against her ex-boyfriend because he was harrassing her at work.

A) restraining

B) against

C) because

D) harrassing

14. Bystanders were noticably upset after witnessing such a horrific accident.

A) Bystanders

B) noticably

C) horrific

D) accident

15. Jason was arrested because he was in possesion of stolen property.

A) arrested

B) because

C) possesion

D) property

INDUCTIVE REASONING

Read the graph below to answer questions 1 – 5.

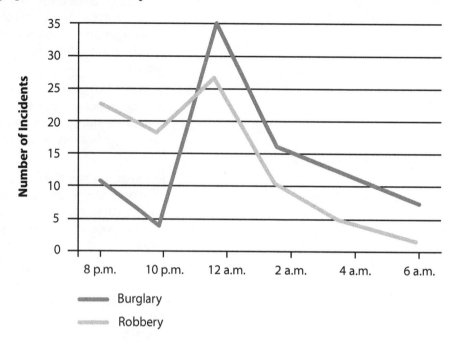

1. Some law enforcement officials blame an increase in all nightly crimes on the local bars closing at the same time. If this spike in crime is related to intoxicated patrons leaving the bars, what is the MOST LIKELY time that all the bars close?

   A) 12:00 a.m.
   B) 1:00 a.m.
   C) 2:00 a.m.
   D) 3:00 a.m.

2. Crime decreases at the sharpest rate during the night when the most police officers are on duty. In which time frame are most police officers MOST LIKELY patrolling?

   A) between 8:00 p.m. and 10:00 p.m.
   B) between 10:00 p.m. and 12:00 a.m.
   C) between 12:00 a.m. and 2:00 a.m.
   D) between 2:00 a.m. and 4:00 a.m.

3. Officer Wilkins can begin his shift anytime between 8:00 p.m. and 6:00 a.m. He wants to start at a time when robberies and burglaries are, on average, at their lowest. Which is the BEST time for the start of Officer Wilkins's shift?

   A) 8:00 p.m.
   B) 10:00 p.m.
   C) 4:00 a.m.
   D) 6:00 a.m.

4. A shift change occurs between 8:00 p.m. and 12:00 a.m., during which criminal activity temporarily decreases. Which of the following is MOST LIKELY the start time of this shift change?

   A) 8:00 p.m.
   B) 9:00 p.m.
   C) 10:00 p.m.
   D) 11:00 p.m.

5. Part-time officers have been hired to help out with the night shift. They can work any four-hour shift between 8:00 p.m. and 6:00 a.m. Which shift would encounter the FEWEST burglaries and robberies, on average?

A) 8:00 p.m. to 12:00 a.m.

B) 10:00 p.m. to 2:00 a.m.

C) 12:00 a.m. to 4:00 a.m.

D) 2:00 a.m. to 6:00 a.m.

Questions 6 – 10 refer to the graph below.

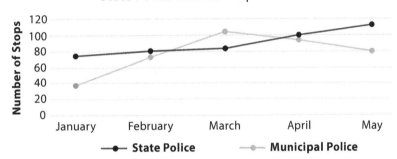

6. Sometime within the first five months of the year, Sergeant Michaels of the state police began an experimental initiative to maintain a quota of around eighty stops per month. What is the MOST LIKELY time frame for this quota?

A) January through March

B) February through April

C) March through April

D) February through May

7. Fearing the spring thaw might lead to an increase in speeding, the state police and municipal police began working together in Washington County to maintain a quota of around one hundred stops. In which month did this joint effort MOST LIKELY take place?

A) February

B) March

C) April

D) May

8. In an effort to "get on the same page" regarding the county's speeding issues, the state police and municipal police collaborated on plans to conduct speeding stops for two out of the first five months. Which two months show the greatest amount of collaboration btween the state police and municipal police?

A) January and February

B) February and May

C) January and April

D) February and April

9. State patrol stops climbed to an all-time high during one of the first five months of the year because a fugitive was on the loose in Washington County. Which month MOST LIKELY represents this scenario?

A) February

B) March

C) April

D) May

10. An unexpected severe blizzard, which led to a state of emergency, was responsible for a five-month low for municipal stops. In which month did this blizzard MOST LIKELY occur?

A) January

B) February

C) March

D) April

Refer to the graph below to answer questions 11 – 15.

State Patrol DUI Statistics

11. After noticing an all-time high of DUI incidents, state police began a new campaign to implement more DUI checkpoints, which led to a sharp decrease in DUIs. In which month did this initiative MOST LIKELY begin?

A) July

B) August

C) September

D) October

12. A sergeant in the state police force is gathering data for a news report about the results of the DUI checkpoint initiative. The sergeant wants to show the total decrease from the highest to lowest number of DUI cases as evidence of the initiative's effectiveness. What is the CLOSEST representation of the total decrease in incidents, according to the graph above?

A) an eighteen-incident decrease

B) a twenty-incident decrease

C) a twenty-four-incident decrease

D) a thirty-two-incident decrease

13. When were the most DUI incidents?

A) July

B) August

C) September

D) October

14. The state patrol set a goal to reduce DUI incidents below eighty. When did the state patrol MOST LIKELY focus on this goal?

A) July

B) August

C) September

D) October

15. A checkpoint off Interstate 94 was implemented for two out of the four months, leading to more consistent data on the number of DUIs. When was this checkpoint MOST LIKELY implemented?

A) July and August

B) July and September

C) August and September

D) September and October

DEDUCTIVE REASONING

Questions 1 – 3 refer to the following passage.

Section 10. Whenever a police officer is ordered to appear before a board of captains as directed by the chief in accordance to State Code, the following procedures shall apply:

1. The hearing shall be conducted at a reasonable hour, and the officer shall receive proper notice to appear.
2. The hearing shall take place either in the chief's conference room or an equivalent setting as designated by the board of captains.
3. Prior to such hearing, the officer shall be provided a Statement of Rights.
4. Hearing sessions shall be for reasonable periods of time and shall allow for personal necessities and rest periods as are reasonably necessary.
5. The board of captains hearing shall be tape-recorded upon the request of either party.

Upon entering the precinct at 7:00 a.m. after his overnight shift, Officer Hallick is notified verbally that he must appear immediately before a board of captains for an administrative meeting. When Officer Hallick enters the room, the board of captains begin questioning him about his relationship with another officer who is being investigated. After two hours of interrogation without any substantial breaks, Officer Hallick demands that the rest of the session be recorded. One of the captains says, "Sorry, Hallick, that is just not going to happen today."

1. According to the sequence of events discussed above, how many of the articles listed in Section 10 of the State Code were violated?

   A) two
   B) three
   C) four
   D) five

Officer Jenson received an official, written notification that she would have to appear before the board of captains for an investigative administrative meeting in fourteen business days. Officer Jenson appeared at the meeting, which took place in the chief's conference room. The board of captains began interrogating Officer Jenson immediately after she entered the room. After the first question, Officer Jenson paused, requesting that the meeting be recorded. The board agreed. The meeting lasted one hour, with two five-minute breaks. An official copy of the tape was placed on record.

2. According to the sequence of events discussed above, how many of the articles listed in Section 10 of the State Code were violated?

   A) none
   B) one
   C) two
   D) three

Officer Wilson received an official, written notification that he would have to appear before the board of captains for an investigative administrative meeting in seven business days. Officer Wilson appeared at the meeting, which took place in the chief's conference room. The board of captains began interrogating Officer Wilson immediately after explaining that the meeting would be taped and reading the Statement of Rights. The meeting lasted two hours, with two thirty-minute breaks. An official copy of the tape was placed on record.

3. According to the sequence of events discussed above, how many of the articles listed in Section 10 of the State Code were violated?

A) none

B) one

C) two

D) three

Questions 4 – 8 refer to the following table.

The merit board has recently reviewed and revised the Disciplinary Code at the Metropolitan Police Department. The Disciplinary Code now reads as follows:

Index of Disciplinary Consequences, 2019 – 2020	
Written Warning to Suspension	▪ Excessive loitering during work hours ▪ Inefficiency or insubordination in the workplace
Written Warning to Discharge	▪ Excessive absenteeism or tardiness ▪ Abuse of the Metropolitan Police Department's property, tools, or materials ▪ Conduct that reflects unfavorably on the Metropolitan Police Department ▪ Falsification of records (including material omission of information) ▪ Offensive conduct or language in the workplace ▪ Discriminatory actions ▪ Falsification of time sheets or department reimbursements ▪ Abusing the sick leave policy (or any other related policy) ▪ Harassment in the workplace ▪ Intoxicated while on the job
Suspension to Discharge	▪ Refusal to participate in a department-authorized physical examination when asked ▪ Participation in political activities while on duty ▪ Repeated rule violations or infractions ▪ Unauthorized use of weapons
Automatic Discharge	Membership in an anti-government institution or revolutionary group that threatens to overthrow the US government
Compulsory Resignation	▪ Three (3) consecutive absences without administrative approval ▪ Felony offense

4. Officer Boyer has been loitering in the precinct during work hours, which has reduced his productivity. According to the list above, what is the MOST severe disciplinary action Officer Boyer can receive for his actions?

A) written warning

B) suspension

C) discharge

D) compulsory resignation

5. Following an investigation, Officer Hampton is found to be a part of an extremist group that is seeking to overthrow the US government. According to protocol, what is the necessary disciplinary action?

A) written warning

B) suspension

C) discharge

D) compulsory resignation

6. Officer Murray is caught accidentally bringing her hunting rifle, an unauthorized firearm, on county property. According to protocol, what is the LEAST severe disciplinary action Officer Murray can receive?

A) written warning

B) suspension

C) discharge

D) compulsory resignation

7. Officer Romero did not show up to duty for three days in a row. His leave was not administratively authorized. According to protocol, what is the necessary disciplinary action?

A) written warning

B) suspension

C) discharge

D) compulsory resignation

8. Officer Gordon is written up for insubordination. This is his first disciplinary action, as he is usually on good standing with his supervisors. What is the MOST LIKELY disciplinary action?

A) written warning

B) suspension

C) discharge

D) compulsory resignation

Questions 9 – 11 refer to the following excerpt.

Section 198-212, The Rules and Regulations of the Metropolitan Police Concerning Disciplinary Action

1. It is mandatory that all disciplinary matters within the agency maintain the rules and regulations established by the merit board in consultation with the chief of police.

2. There are four possible disciplinary actions that can be delivered once an infraction is fully investigated:
   □ documented warning
   □ suspension (without pay)
   □ demotion in merit rank
   □ termination and discharge

3. Agency members believed to be in violation of a board-approved rule or regulation can be placed on administrative leave, with pay, for up to forty-five (45) calendar days by the chief of police, pending a thorough internal investigation and determination by the Internal Investigations Department. This initial leave will not be considered a punishment; rather, it will be defined as normal agency procedure.

4. While the Internal Investigations Department will carry out a thorough investigation and offer a determination, the authority to discipline an agency subordinate ultimately rests solely within the power of the chief of police. Following the investigation, the chief can choose to:

- issue a documented warning, which will be filed for future consideration within an agency member's Human Resources file.
- suspend the officer, without pay, anywhere from a minimum of seven (7) calendar days to a maximum of three (3) calendar months.
  - Whenever an agency member is suspended without pay, they may appeal this disciplinary action within one (1) month of their suspension.
- demote the agency member and lower their merit rank by no more than one (1) official rank.
  - Whenever an agency member is demoted, they may appeal this disciplinary action within one (1) month of their demotion.
- recommend that the agency member be terminated and discharged from their duties.
  - Any recommendation for termination and discharge must first be taken to an administrative hearing.

9. Officer Stevens broke one of the department rules and regulations established by the chief, merit board, and Department of Public Safety. Chief Carter places Officer Stevens on leave, without pay, for forty-five calendar days. Unsure of how to handle the matter, the chief refers the case to a disciplinary board of captains for recommendation. The board recommends suspending the officer for nine calendar days. The chief follows this advice, deciding to suspend Officer Stevens for nine calendar days without pay.

   According to the sequence of events discussed above, what grounds might Officer Stevens have for an appeal?

   A) the number of days of suspension warrants such an appeal

   B) he should have been placed on leave *with* pay

   C) he only broke one rule or regulation

   D) he did not receive a written reprimand

10. Officer Leon broke one of the agency's rules and regulations, so Chief Armstrong places her on leave with pay for forty-five calendar days. The chief refers the case to a disciplinary board of captains for recommendation. The board recommends suspending the officer for three calendar months. The chief follows this advice, deciding to suspend Officer Leon for three calendar months without pay.

    According to the sequence of events discussed above, what grounds might Officer Leon have for an appeal?

    A) any suspension without pay can be appealed

    B) she was placed on leave without pay

    C) she only broke one rule or regulation

    D) she did not receive a written reprimand

11. If Officer Leon was notified of a demotion, how many months would she have to appeal?

    A) one

    B) three

    C) nine

    D) twelve

Questions 12 and 13 refer to the following excerpt on unattended vehicles.

When a police officer arrives at an unattended vehicle during a routine patrol, he or she should adhere to the following protocols:

1. notify radio dispatch about the location and description of vehicle
2. call a tow truck to remove the vehicle, if necessary
3. ask radio dispatch to run the license plate (if there is one on the car) to determine if the car has been reported stolen
4. try to contact the vehicle's owner(s)
5. make a log of all actions and communications in an activity log

12. Officer Morrison is on a routine patrol when she observes an abandoned vehicle parked on the side of a highway, presenting a danger to commuters. She communicates the vehicle's location and description to radio dispatch and calls for a tow truck. After running the license plate, radio dispatch reports that the car is not reported stolen. What is Officer Morrison's next step?

A) report to a ranking officer about the location of the car
B) contact the vehicle's owner(s)
C) make a log of all actions and communications in an activity log
D) make note of the make, model, and color of the vehicle

13. Officer McNamara notices an abandoned vehicle in the parking lot of a state park after the park has closed. The car is not obstructing traffic. No rules are posted about vehicle parked after hours. He radios dispatch about the location of the car; provides the make, model, and color of the vehicle; and runs the license plate. Next, he notes all communications in an activity log. According to the protocols above, what step did Officer McNamara forget to take?

A) call a tow truck
B) provide a description of the vehicle to radio dispatch
C) make a note of all actions and communications in an activity log
D) try to contact the vehicle's owner(s)

Questions 14 – 15 refer to the following excerpt on procedures for intoxicated drivers.

If an officer believes a motorist is driving under the influence of alcohol, the officer should follow these procedures:

1. Issue a separate citation for any original traffic offense (i.e., speeding).
2. Confiscate the driver's license if they take a blood alcohol test and score over the legal limit (the officer also reserves the right to confiscate a driver's license if they refuse to take a blood alcohol test).
3. Do not confiscate the driver's license if the driver takes a blood alcohol test and does NOT exceed the legal limit of intoxication. Officers may still implement field sobriety assessments if they suspect that the driver is intoxicated.
4. Even if a blood alcohol test does not exceed the legal limit, the officer maintains the right to validate a DUI charge if the person fails a set of field sobriety assessments.

14. Officer White issues a ticket for reckless driving to a motorist whose car was swerving on the highway. She then asks the driver to take a blood alcohol test. The driver is under the legal limit of alcohol consumption and passes the test. However, Officer White still believes the driver may be intoxicated and under the influence of alcohol.

What is the next appropriate step for Officer White?

   A) make the driver submit to another blood alcohol test

   B) confiscate the driver's license

   C) issue a citation for driving under the influence of alcohol

   D) carry out a field sobriety assessment

15. Officer Del Rio pulls over a speeding SUV and issues the driver a speeding ticket. However, he suspects that the driver is intoxicated. He asks the driver to take a blood alcohol test. The driver refuses.

What is the next appropriate step for Officer Del Rio?

   A) confiscate the driver's license

   B) carry out field sobriety assessments

   C) call for backup

   D) make the driver take the blood alcohol test

INFORMATION ORDERING

Officer Bailey responds to a recent assault on the boardwalk in Atlantic City, New Jersey. He receives the following testimony from the victim:

1. I bought some cotton candy right by the boardwalk and began taking a peaceful stroll.
2. I just got off my shift at the local restaurant when I decided to buy some cotton candy and go for a walk on the boardwalk.
3. He asked for some money.
4. A vagrant—he was about five foot six, frail, shirtless, and with a gray beard—approached me about thirty minutes into my walk.
5. I refused to give him any money.
6. When I refused his request, he grabbed me by the throat before a Good Samaritan scared him off.

1. What is the MOST logical order for the steps listed above?
   A) 2, 1, 4, 3, 5, 6
   B) 1, 6, 3, 5, 4, 2
   C) 2, 1, 5, 6, 3, 4
   D) 1, 2, 6, 5, 3, 4

Officer Morales just interviewed the victim of an assault and robbery. The following statements appeared in the victim's testimony about the incident:

1. I ran into my backyard after breaking free from his grip.
2. He tried to grab my arm, but I escaped.
3. I rounded the corner of William Cannon and Salt Springs Drive near my home.
4. As I rounded the corner, I saw Daniel Davidson, my brother's friend.
5. I did not want to interact with Daniel because he looked like he was "speeding" on narcotics.
6. He snatched my purse while I was on the ground and I began to cry.
7. A neighbor heard me crying.
8. Daniel chased me into my backyard and tackled me to the ground.
9. The neighbor chased Daniel away.
10. Daniel refused to let me pass even though I was ignoring him.

2. The victim is agitated and describing the events out of order. Which statements logically describe the FIRST five events in the testimony?
   A) 4, 1, 2, 10, 3
   B) 3, 4, 5, 10, 2
   C) 5, 3, 4, 9, 7
   D) 2, 8, 6, 7, 9

3. Which statements logically describe the SECOND five events in this testimony?
   A) 1, 8, 6, 7, 9
   B) 2, 8, 6, 7, 9
   C) 3, 4, 5, 10, 2
   D) 10, 2, 3, 5, 9

When transporting a person placed under arrest, these protocols should be followed (note: these protocols are not listed in the correct order):

1. handcuff the person
2. place the person in the back of the police cruiser
3. notify radio dispatch of the arrest
4. carry out a wingspan search for weapons, narcotics, or other illicit items

4. What is the MOST logical order for the protocols above?
   A) 4, 1, 2, 3
   B) 1, 3, 2, 4
   C) 2, 4, 3, 1
   D) 3, 1, 2, 4

A police officer goes to a local gas station to gather information about a recent crime. The following details were taken from witness testimonies:

1. The two men escaped through a side door just after the police told them to stop.
2. One of the men pointed a gun at me, and ordered that I hand over the cash from the cash register.
3. The police came into the gas station and attempted to deter the two men from escaping.
4. Two masked men entered the gas station.
5. I handed over the cash just as the police made it to the scene.

5. What is the MOST logical order for the events described above?
   A) 1, 3, 2, 4, 5
   B) 4, 2, 5, 3, 1
   C) 2, 3, 4, 1, 5
   D) 2, 4, 5, 3, 1

A police officer reports to the scene of a recent stabbing. The witnesses give the following details in their testimonies:

1. The woman's brother, the owner of the bar, monitored it for a bit, and stepped outside with a sharp object in his hand that looked like a tool or ice pick "when he could not take it anymore."
2. A man and a woman were arguing outside a bar.
3. The brother threatened to stab the man.
4. He jabbed a sharp object into the man's abdomen.
5. They were arguing so forcefully that it got the attention of everyone in the bar, including the woman's brother, the owner of the bar.

6. What is the MOST logical order for the events described above?
   A) 5, 2, 3, 1, 4
   B) 4, 3, 2, 1, 5
   C) 2, 5, 1, 3, 4
   D) 2, 1, 5, 3, 4

A police officer arrives at the scene of a car burglary. The officer receives the following details from a local resident:

1. I saw an old man park his car and go into the school.
2. The old man came out of the school when he heard the window breaking.
3. He used the tool to break the window.
4. As soon as he walked through the door, a young man wearing a red hooded sweatshirt turned the corner and approached the car with a tool in his hand.
5. He yelled at the young man for breaking into his car, and the young man ran down Eleventh Street with an iPhone in his hand.

7. What is the MOST logical order for the events described above?
   A) 1, 2, 3, 4, 5
   B) 1, 4, 5, 2, 3
   C) 1, 4, 3, 2, 5
   D) 5, 1, 2, 3, 4

Police officers must not only stop crime; they must also know how to treat those who are critically injured at crime scenes. Some injuries a police officer might encounter include:

1. shock
2. heart failure
3. deep wound bleeding
4. non-protruding broken bone
5. minor lacerations

8. A victim of a crime is affected by all of these injuries, and an ambulance has not yet arrived. In what order should a police officer treat these injuries?
   A) 2, 3, 1, 4, 5
   B) 5, 4, 1, 3, 2
   C) 4, 5, 1, 2, 3
   D) 5, 3, 2, 1, 4

A police officer arrives at the scene of an arson incident. While interviewing several witnesses to the crime, the officer receives the following statements:

1. Sandy Gomez saw two teenagers running with some fireworks toward an alleyway.
2. The teenagers ignored her question and ran into the alleyway.
3. She yelled at the teenagers, "Hey, where are you going?" immediately after she saw them running toward the alleyway.
4. About two minutes later, she heard glass breaking and a big booming sound.
5. Seconds after she heard these sounds, she noticed the smoke and flames coming from a garage in the alleyway.
6. She saw the teens run off from the smoke and flames, and that is when she called 911.

9. What is the MOST logical order for the events described above?

    A) 1, 3, 2, 4, 5, 6

    B) 5, 1, 3, 2, 4, 6

    C) 1, 2, 3, 4, 5, 6

    D) 5, 4, 6, 2, 3, 1

Officer Atkins, a police officer at the University of Richmond, arrives at the scene of a vandalism attempt. Atkins receives the following testimonies from witnesses:

    1. We showed up late to the protest. By the time we got there, it was already pretty out of control. From far away, we could see the flames of a bonfire that had been started near the controversial statue on campus.

    2. The police arrived just as the first statue tumbled to the ground. The protesters scattered.

    3. Before you knew it, the fire was reaching twenty feet in height, and the statue was starting to collapse from the impact.

    4. As we got closer to the fire, we noticed three masked protesters damaging not only the controversial statue in the park but other statues as well. They were using sledgehammers to break the concrete foundations.

10. What is the MOST logical order for the events described above?

    A) 1, 2, 3, 4

    B) 2, 4, 3, 1

    C) 1, 4, 3, 2

    D) 3, 4, 1, 2

11. What is the MOST LIKELY reason that the protesters scattered?

    A) The fire got out of control.

    B) The statue began to collapse.

    C) The police arrived.

    D) The protest was over.

Officer Garrison is interviewing Betty Stonelake about an armed robbery she witnessed at a local convenience store. The following statements appear in her testimony:

    1. I went to the back of the store to pick up a half gallon of milk.

    2. That's when I saw the man pull a gun on the cashier and ask for money.

    3. I dropped quietly to the ground and waited until I heard the man leave. I knew he was gone because I heard the bells on the door.

    4. On my way to the cash register to pay for the milk, I noticed a suspicious man walk into the store.

    5. I entered the store at about 3:00 a.m.

12. What is the MOST logical order for the events described above?

    A) 1, 5, 4, 2, 3

    B) 4, 2, 3, 1, 5

    C) 5, 1, 4, 2, 3

    D) 1, 4, 2, 3, 5

Detective Harper is interviewing Tara Schmidt, a bartender at a local bar. Ms. Schmidt says that she witnessed an assault on a patron named Bruce Houser. The following statements appear in her testimony:

1. I know that one of the men was Bruce Houser, but I do not know the name of the other man. I noticed them arguing for a bit before I saw the other man push Bruce.
2. I was about midway through my shift when I noticed two men arguing near the restroom.
3. The man exited the side door after the assault.
4. I called the police when the man left because Bruce looked unconscious.
5. At that point, Bruce fell and hit his head on the radiator.

13. What is the MOST logical order for the events described above?

   A) 3, 2, 1, 4, 5

   B) 1, 2, 5, 3, 4

   C) 2, 1, 5, 3, 4

   D) 2, 1, 5, 4, 3

You are at a local outdoor shooting range to test your new firearm. As you enter the shooting range, you must review a checklist of the facility's procedures and expectations, which follow (not in order):

1. Facility-approved ear protection must be acquired at the front desk and worn before entering the firing zone.
2. Reloading of any firearm should be done outside of the firing area.
3. Return all ear protection equipment to the front desk before leaving.
4. Firearms must be registered and placed on safety before they can be brought into the facility.
5. Firearms must once again be placed on safety after completion of firing practice.
6. Firearms can be taken off safety immediately prior to firing, once the officer reaches their specific firing area. The officer can proceed to fire at this time.

14. What is the MOST logical order for this checklist?

   A) 4, 1, 6, 2, 5, 3

   B) 3, 1, 2, 5, 4, 6

   C) 6, 1, 4, 3, 2, 5

   D) 5, 3, 2, 1, 6, 4

You went to a local fast-food restaurant to gather information about a crime. The following statements were taken from a witness about an attempted robbery:

1. I was ordered to give the masked woman my jewelry and purse.
2. Two masked men and one masked woman entered the fast-food restaurant.
3. I remained on the scene to provide law enforcement with my statement.
4. I handed my earrings, wedding ring, and purse to the masked woman.
5. The three masked individuals fled through the side door when the first responding police officer arrived.

15. What is the MOST logical order for the events described above?

   A) 1, 2, 3, 5, 4

   B) 4, 2, 3, 5, 1

   C) 2, 3, 4, 5, 1

   D) 2, 1, 4, 5, 3

PROBLEM SENSITIVITY

Officer Singh has been observing the behavior and attitude of Officer Brown, a new police officer. Singh has noticed that Brown is usually calm and happy but sometimes appears to be restless and anxious. At first, Singh thought the mood swings stemmed from issues at home, but then he started to notice Brown's behavior becoming more erratic. Singh asked Brown if everything was okay at home. He noticed Brown's pupils were dilated, his eyes were bloodshot, and his hands were shaking. Brown snapped at Singh, telling him to "leave him alone." Singh saw Brown with what appeared to be pills in a plastic bag in Brown's locker. When Brown saw Singh, he concealed the bag. Later that day, Brown apologized to Singh for being rude. He told Singh that everything was okay at home and not to worry. Singh was not convinced by his statement.

1. What is MOST LIKELY causing Brown's erratic behavior?

A) family problems

B) financial issues

C) drug use

D) job stress

2. What is the most suspicious observation made by Officer Singh?

A) Brown's mood swings

B) Brown's bloodshot eyes

C) Brown's apology

D) Brown's bag of pills

3. What is the MOST LIKELY reason that Officer Brown apologized to Officer Singh?

A) He felt bad for being rude.

B) He wanted to put Singh at ease after being caught with pills.

C) He got in trouble with a superior officer for his behavior.

D) He was encouraged to apologize by his family.

Officer Keating is investigating an attempted robbery near Giant Grocery Store, reported via a 911 call by a store clerk, Kelly Zicchardo. Officer Keating is at the Giant Grocery Store interviewing witnesses. The following information is from witness statements:

Harry Cartwright, the victim of the attempted robbery, states that he was going to Giant Grocery Store to buy a pack of cigarettes when a homeless man accosted him, asking him for money. Cartwright says it was a little after 7:00 p.m. because he remembers hearing the local church bells ringing a few minutes earlier, and they ring every day at that time. When Cartwright refused to give the money, the panhandler, who seemed skittish, tried to threaten him with a knife. Cartwright laughed the situation off, saying, "Oh, you've got to be kidding me." But before he could finish his comment, the man had him pinned to the curb outside the store. Cartwright hit his head on the curb. Around that time, Cartwright saw Jim Lord, a fellow customer, pull out a licensed, concealed firearm. He pointed the gun at the panhandler, shouting, "Drop your weapon!" Kelly Zicchardo emerged from the store, shouting, "I'm calling the police!" That is when Cartwright felt the man release his grip.

John Albright, a twenty-six-year-old customer who was parked in the parking lot at the time of the incident, claims the homeless man had previously solicited him for drugs and money. Albright, who claims to be "street savvy," says the homeless man looked a bit paranoid, asking him for "a fix or some cash." He also says the man's name is Michael Coatesville, and he is known to be a local addict with a history of violence. Albright says he did not see the incident, but he stopped his car when he heard a commotion near the door's entrance.

Kelly Zicchardo, a forty-five-year-old cashier, says she did not see much because everything happened so fast. She says she had just clocked in for her 7:00 p.m. shift when she heard someone shout, "Drop your weapon!" She remembers looking at the cash register, and it said 7:07 p.m. That is when she ran out, shouting, "I'm calling the police!"

Jim Lord, a twenty-three-year-old military veteran, says he was just going to the grocery store after his twelve-hour shift at Reading Anthracite. His shift ended at 6:45 p.m. and it usually took him around twenty minutes to get to the store. He remembers pulling up to the store at 7:05 p.m. He claims he was just grabbing a shopping cart when he saw a homeless man draw his knife on another man. He says he was trained in the military to handle these situations, and he felt the man was enough of a threat to draw his licensed firearm. He says he was "just trying to be a good citizen," and he did not get a good look at the man's face, but he definitely scared him off.

4. What time did Jim Lord MOST LIKELY try to intervene in the robbery?

A) 6:45 p.m.

B) 7:00 p.m.

C) 7:05 p.m.

D) 7:07 p.m.

5. Which witness is MOST LIKELY to provide the most reliable details about the crime?

A) Officer Keating

B) Kelly Zicchardo

C) John Albright

D) Jim Lord

6. According to the testimonies taken, what was likely the intent of the attempted robbery?

A) to get money for drugs

B) to rob the cash register

C) to get money for food

D) to buy a pack of cigarettes

Officer Crawley must respond to a prowler call at Sixteenth and Center Streets. He is the first officer to arrive at the scene and waits for backup in his patrol car. A civilian approaches the officer. The civilian matches the description of the suspected prowler. The civilian complains that the patrol car is in his neighborhood, taking up perfectly good parking spaces. He asks Officer Crawley what the problem is and offers to help search the neighborhood for any suspicious activity because he is part of the Neighborhood Watch program.

7. Which of the following is the MOST appropriate action for Officer Crawley to take in this situation?

A) send the civilian on a quick mission to search the vicinity and, if necessary, join the search

B) arrest the civilian immediately for prowling

C) radio for immediate backup just in case the civilian is the actual prowler

D) engage the civilian in conversation to decide whether he is the suspect

The following are the statements of witnesses concerning four different arson incidents.

WITNESS 1: Jack Cho was on his way to work when he noticed a young man running away from a building. A moment later, he noticed the building was in flames. The young man was tall and very thin.

WITNESS 2: Kirk Browning was drinking coffee in his kitchen when he looked out the window and saw the house across the street on fire. He ran to the back door. When he looked out from his back door, he saw a group of teenagers running away from the building.

WITNESS 3: Troy Saunders was working outside when he saw flames coming from an office window. He then saw a man in his forties quickly driving away in his car.

WITNESS 4: Arnie Haynes was going to the local bar when he heard a man screaming that his house was on fire. He noticed a tall, young man running away from the scene.

8. Which two witnesses MOST LIKELY saw the same arsonist, according to the information above?
   A) Jack Cho and Troy Saunders
   B) Kirk Browning and Troy Saunders
   C) Jack Cho and Arnie Haynes
   D) Kirk Browning and Arnie Haynes

Officer Gordon responds to an incident at Mrs. Pilconis's home. She tells him that her black 2019 Ford Expedition has been stolen, claiming that the last time she saw it was when she parked it across the street from her house at 2:00 a.m. After completing the interview, Officer Gordon returns to his squad car to prepare his report, in which he writes that Mrs. Pilconis reported that her black SUV was stolen. He also writes that the vehicle was last seen at 2:00 a.m. across the street from her house where she parked it.

9. What did Officer Gordon forget to report?
   A) the time the vehicle was last seen
   B) the last known location of the vehicle
   C) the color of the vehicle
   D) the make and model of the vehicle

Officer Brenner is conducting a routine patrol of a neighborhood where a string of burglaries has recently taken place. She notices that a suspicious-looking man wearing dark clothing matches the description of the man reported to be involved in the burglaries. The man is moving quickly past her patrol car, refusing to make eye contact and staring at the ground.

10. What should Officer Brenner do?
   A) draw her weapon and tell the man to lie on the ground
   B) interview neighbors for their testimonies
   C) continue her routine patrol of the neighborhood
   D) stop the man and ask him what is going on

A fellow officer regularly gets into irrational arguments with citizens while on patrol. Most of the time the incidents are minor and no one notices. However, at other times, his behavior reflects poorly on the department. After witnessing a particularly troubling situation, his partner feels like something must be said about the officer's behavior.

11. How should the partner handle the situation?
   A) apologize to citizens when he berates them in public
   B) speak to the commanding officer, since it is not his duty to discipline the officer
   C) speak to the officer in private to explain the consequences of his behavior
   D) ignore the behavior since, as his peer, there is nothing he can do

Officer Bailey interviewed four witnesses to a bank robbery. Each one described the suspects as follows:

WITNESS 1: "Both men had on gray slacks, black dress shoes, and suit coats. One coat was gray, the other was black. One of the men had long blond hair. The other man's hair was not visible because he had a Halloween mask on. They both looked short—less than six feet tall. The man with the mask was the only one who spoke."

WITNESS 2: "Both of the men were about the same size. They were short—certainly less than six feet tall, and neither could've weighed more than 175 pounds. One of them was wearing a black suit coat, and the other one was wearing a gray suit coat. I couldn't see their faces. One had a Halloween mask on. The other one, the one with long blond hair, was wearing a green bandana over his face."

WITNESS 3: "Both of the men were tall. Both had suit coats on. They were also wearing blue jeans and tennis shoes. One had blond hair with a bandana. The other one was wearing some kind of mask. Neither of them spoke."

WITNESS 4: "There were two people involved. Both were men. They were short for men. Less than six feet tall. They had slim builds. One of them had long blond hair. He was wearing a green bandana, gray slacks, and a gray suit coat. The other had a black suit coat. He was wearing a Halloween mask, so I could not see his hair. Only the one with the Halloween mask spoke. His voice sounded muffled, but he sounded like he had an accent."

12. Which witness's testimony is MOST LIKELY flawed?

    A) Witness 1

    B) Witness 2

    C) Witness 3

    D) Witness 4

You and your partner respond to a domestic assault incident involving a male suspect. When the suspect is detained, he kicks your partner. Your partner spits on the suspect while in custody.

13. What is the MOST appropriate way to handle this situation?

    A) report the incident to his supervisor without an initial conversation

    B) tell your partner that his behavior was inappropriate and remind him that if it happens again it must be reported

    C) tell the officer that his behavior was inappropriate and that he needs to tell his supervisor or else you will have to report it

    D) ignore the incident because the spitting was reactionary to the suspect's violent behavior

You and your partner arrive at a house where a burglary is reported to be occurring. As you approach the house you hear a woman scream in the backyard. The gate is open. You hear a man yell, "Shut up or I'll kill you!" You also hear a warning shot fired in the air. Your partner is visibly anxious and asks, "What should we do?"

14. What is the MOST appropriate way to handle this situation?

    A) radio dispatch to see if it is the correct house before acting

    B) tell your partner to stay in the car so you can knock on the door

    C) try to enter the backyard and contact a supervisor after the situation is under control

    D) wait for your supervisor's permission to enter the building

You are patrolling a neighborhood with your partner in a patrol car. He initiates a traffic stop on a sedan with a broken taillight. The driver of the sedan refuses to stop and speeds away from the patrol car. You radio dispatch to inform your team that you are pursuing a vehicle that disregarded a routine traffic stop and is now speeding. Your shift supervisor instructs you to cancel the pursuit.

15. What is the MOST appropriate way to handle this situation?

    A) confirm that you understand the order and stop following the sedan

    B) ignore your supervisor's order and continue following the sedan

    C) radio another police officer to continue the pursuit on your behalf

    D) radio your supervisor to cancel the order and continue the pursuit

SPATIAL ORIENTATION

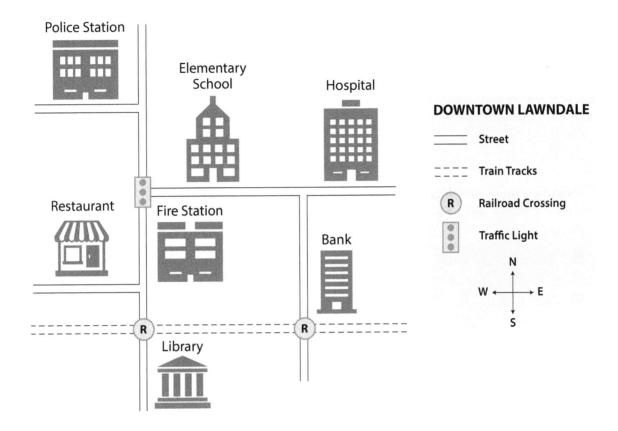

Police Station

Elementary School

Hospital

DOWNTOWN LAWNDALE

—— Street

- - - - Train Tracks

(R) Railroad Crossing

Traffic Light

Restaurant

Fire Station

Bank

Library

N
W ← → E
S

Officer Willis is currently parked in front of the police station, getting ready for his shift, when he receives radio confirmation about a bank robbery. He decides to drive to the scene of the crime, since the bank is far from the police station.

1. How many intersections will Officer Willis encounter on his way to the bank?
   - **A)** one
   - **B)** two
   - **C)** three
   - **D)** four

2. How many right-hand turns will Officer Willis make on the way to the bank?
   - **A)** one
   - **B)** two
   - **C)** three
   - **D)** four

Officer Willis is parked at the library and has to respond to an incident at the hospital.

3. How many times will Officer Willis have to cross the railroad tracks on his way to the hospital?
   - **A)** none
   - **B)** one
   - **C)** two
   - **D)** three

4. How many left-hand turns will Officer Willis make?
   - **A)** none
   - **B)** one
   - **C)** two
   - **D)** three

Officer Willis's new patrol route starts at the police station, makes a U-turn in front of the library, makes another a U-turn in front of the hospital, crosses the railroad tracks by the bank, makes another U-turn, and returns to the police station.

5. How many times will Officer Willis pass the streetlight on a single patrol?

    A) one

    B) two

    C) three

    D) four

6. How many times will Officer Willis cross the train tracks on a single patrol?

    A) one

    B) two

    C) three

    D) four

7. How many times will Officer Willis pass the bank on a single patrol?

    A) one

    B) two

    C) three

    D) four

Whitney Parkway

Lake Whitney

Chestnut Point Road

Lakeview Highway

LAKE WHITNEY HIGHWAYS

——— Residential Street

- - - - Two-Lane Highway

═══ Four-Lane Highway

N
W — E
S

1 mile

Officer Klinger is heading eastbound on Whitney Parkway, just west of Lake Whitney. She is ordered to investigate a car crash on Lakeview Highway, about a mile west of the intersection between Lakeview Highway and Chestnut Point Road, just south of Lake Whitney.

8. How many right-hand turns will Officer Klinger make in order to arrive at the scene of the crash?

    A) none

    B) one

    C) two

    D) three

9. How many left-hand turns will Officer Klinger make in order to arrive at the scene of the crash?

    A) none

    B) one

    C) two

    D) three

The Lake Whitney residential community is south of Whitney Parkway, west of Chestnut Point Road, and roughly northeast of the middle of Lake Whitney. Officer Klinger is parked at the intersection of the southernmost road in the Lake Whitney residential neighborhood and Chestnut Point Road. Her car is facing east, monitoring traffic closest to the southbound side of Chestnut Point Road, when she notices a car speeding northbound on Chestnut Point Road. Before she can even get her lights on, she sees the car take a sharp, dangerous right on Whitney Parkway before finally catching up with the vehicle and pulling it over a mile east of the intersection of Whitney Parkway and Chestnut Point Road.

10. How many turns will Officer Klinger make on her route?

A) one

B) two

C) three

D) four

11. Where on the map will Officer Klinger be positioned when she pulls the car over?

A) northeast

B) northwest

C) southeast

D) southwest

12. How many left-hand turns will Officer Klinger make during the pursuit?

A) one

B) two

C) three

D) four

13. How many four-lane highways will Officer Klinger travel on during her pursuit?

A) one

B) two

C) three

D) four

The Lake Whitney map represents the total range of Officer Klinger's jurisdiction. She patrols residential streets, two-lane highways, and four-lane highways.

14. How many residential streets are in Officer Klinger's jurisdiction?

A) eleven

B) twelve

C) thirteen

D) fourteen

15. How many highways are in Officer Klinger's jurisdiction?

A) one

B) two

C) three

D) four

MEMORIZATION

Study each image for up to two minutes. Then, answer the questions using only your memory of what you observed in the image.

Image One

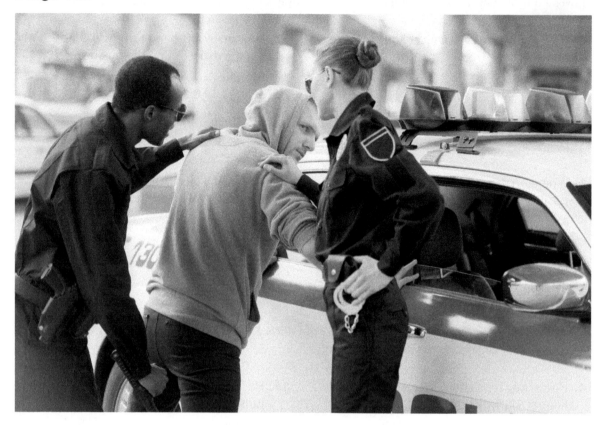

1. What is the suspect in the photograph wearing?

   A) a costume

   B) jeans and a hooded sweatshirt

   C) a jumpsuit

   D) shorts and T-shirt

2. What is the subject leaning against in the photograph?

   A) a wall

   B) a pillar

   C) a fence

   D) a squad car

3. What is the female police officer gripping with her left hand in the photograph?

   A) the suspect

   B) the other police officer's shoulder

   C) handcuffs

   D) the squad car

Image Two

4. What is pictured in the upper left-hand corner of the photograph?

   A) a hubcap

   B) broken glass

   C) caution tape

   D) a person on the ground

5. What number is the officer placing near the crime scene?

   A) 1

   B) 2

   C) 3

   D) 4

6. How many people are pictured in the photograph?

   A) one

   B) two

   C) three

   D) four

Image Three

7. What is the person in the photograph gripping in their right hand?

    A) a gun

    B) a magnifying glass

    C) a brush

    D) a cell phone

8. How many markers are visible on the ground in the photograph?

    A) one

    B) two

    C) three

    D) four

9. What is the presumed location of the crime scene?

    A) a paved city parking lot

    B) a police station

    C) a wooded area

    D) a playground

Image Four

10. What is the police officer on the left MOST LIKELY doing in the photograph?

    A) questioning a suspect

    B) frisking a suspect

    C) detaining a suspect

    D) directing traffic

11. What is the suspect in the photograph kneeling next to?

    A) a squad car

    B) another suspect

    C) a traffic cone

    D) a fence

12. Which way is the suspect's head facing in the photograph?

    A) to the right

    B) to the left

    C) away from the camera

    D) toward the camera

Image Five

13. What does it say on the officer's vest in the photograph?

    A) EVENTS

    B) POLICE

    C) LAPD

    D) NYPD

14. Which direction is the closest car driving in the photograph?

    A) from right to left

    B) from left to right

    C) toward the camera

    D) away from the camera

15. What is the police officer MOST LIKELY doing in the photograph?

    A) detaining a suspect

    B) patrolling in a squad car

    C) directing traffic and pedestrian crossings

    D) securing a crime scene

ANSWER KEY

WRITTEN COMPREHENSION

1. **A) is correct.** The passage is written with an impersonal objective tone, much like an article or news report, rather than to persuade or debate. It is not argumentative, passionate, or empathetic.

2. **A) is correct.** In this context, *imperative* means "absolutely necessary." The passage asserts that "many people do not wish to move beyond this basic, instinctual level" of thought to critical thinking unless they must. It must be essential for them to engage in critical thinking, not just important or interesting (choices B and C). Choice D, *avoidable*, is not relevant here.

3. **D) is correct.** Only I and III are true. Option II, which states critical thinking is *only* important in academia, contradicts the first sentence of paragraph 3: "Since the 1970s, critical thinking has also been used in police work." In fact, the point of the passage is that critical thinking is vital to police work (choice III).

4. **D) is correct.** If fewer crimes were successfully investigated and prosecuted since police began using critical thinking in investigations, then it would appear critical thinking is not helpful in police work. The

purpose of paragraph 3 is to illustrate the many ways critical thinking has been used and can help in law enforcement. Answers A, B, and C are incorrect because they misstate facts or ideas from the passage.

5. **B) is correct.** The definition of *savvy* is *shrewd*. This paragraph states that policing requires critical thinking to outsmart criminals. Choice A, *cool*, is not relevant here. *Inexperienced* is the opposite meaning; a savvy criminal would likely be quite experienced. And *dangerous* criminals are not necessarily savvy.

6. **B) is correct.** The best title for this passage is "Critical Thinking and Law Enforcement." Although the passage defines critical thinking and illustrates its various applications, the bulk of the passage talks about the application of critical thinking to law enforcement. Thus answer B is the best choice.

7. **D) is correct.** Each point was presented as an important reason critical thinking is used in law enforcement.

8. **D) is correct.** The chief's letter identifies personal reasons why many people

cannot schedule exercise into their daily routines. It also mentions the "warriors" who do work out in the morning, and the liability issues around allowing staff to exercise during shifts. Thus, D is the best answer; the chief will help, but he puts the responsibility on the employee to manage his or her time.

9. **A) is correct.** The tone of the letter is cordial. The letter uses mostly friendly and supportive words in a professional format. The chief begins his letter by applauding employees for wanting to meet standards. He clearly explains the reasoning for his own choices in changing policy by taking away food options and prohibiting exercise on meal breaks. While it is debatable whether those choices are good policy for the officers, the tone of the letter is not angry or overbearing, ruling out choices B and D. He does express enthusiasm for the "warriors" he already works out with and says they would "love" other officers to join them, but this is more enthusiastic than passionate, ruling out choice C.

10. **B) is correct.** As used in the passage, the chief implies the "warriors" who work out every morning with him show motivation, energy, and a willingness to do what it takes to fit exercise into their schedules. Warfare and weapons are irrelevant to this passage. Finally, the chief does not suggest that those who work out with him are exceptionally experienced; otherwise, he would not invite those officers looking to improve their fitness to join them.

11. **D) is correct.** The chief notes both logistics and liability as reasons why he denied the request.

12. **C) is correct.** The introduction to the passage states that most officers spend fifteen hours a day working and commuting. There are twenty-four hours in a day; fifteen subtracted from twenty-four leaves nine hours remaining.

13. **A) is correct.** The author's main point is that bullying has increased in scope from years past. If the number of children being bullied has increased, this strengthens the author's argument. The author asserts that bullying occurs beyond school, thanks to technology, making answer choice B incorrect. The passage discusses SROs at length, so if there were less funding for SROs, the argument would be weakened, making C incorrect. Finally, the passage states that youth suicides are increasing, so choice D directly contradicts the passage, making it incorrect.

14. **B) is correct.** According to the passage, "SROs talk to kids at particular schools regularly," so "officers are in a unique position to identify emerging issues and prevent them before they develop into greater problems." The passage never states that SROs arrest bullies, just that SROs "are stationed at the school and spend their time dealing with law enforcement issues." SROs do not offer training; they "receive training in issues that are unique to youth." The passage never states specifically that SROs show teachers how to identify bullies, just that all personnel work together "to ensure schools remain a safe place for kids to learn."

15. **C) is correct.** The passage immediately asserts that technological advancement has made bullying more prevalent. The first paragraph states that "[b]ullying among children and adolescents has evolved…to cyberstalking children across city and state lines with the use of common electronic devices." The passage explains that school resource officers enhance safety at school, so B is not correct. Finally, the passage never mentions more negative behavior among children or boredom as factors in bullying, ruling out answer choices A and D.

WRITTEN EXPRESSION

1. **B) is correct.** *Has* is a singular verb, referring to a singular noun (*Neptune*); *seasons* is the direct object of the verb *has*. *Seasons* must be plural to take the plural verb *last*.

2. **C) is correct.** The plural verb *are* agrees with its plural subject *paintings*. The sentence has no error.

3. **D) is correct.** *Presidential* is an adjective that modifies the common noun *election*; neither word should be capitalized.

4. **B) is correct.** A comma should never separate a subject (*Nile River*) from its verb (*passes*) without an interceding appositive.

5. **A) is correct.** *Grandchildren* and *cousins* are plural and so take the plural pronoun *their*.

6. **D) is correct.** *Mountain's* is not possessive in this sentence. It functions as a plural noun (*mountains*) so it does not require an apostrophe.

7. **B) is correct.** Because the sentence states a general fact (how seat belts work), it should be written in present (or past) tense. The verb must be plural, since its subject, *Engineers*, is plural.

8. **D) is correct.** The sentence already contains a negative ("The employer decided he could not...") so the modifier must be *any*; using a phrase like "no other benefits" would create an incorrect double negative.

9. **B) is correct.** *And also functioned* introduces the second part of a compound verb phrase (*was created and functioned*).

10. **D) is correct.** Choice D is the only correctly punctuated sentence. A comma correctly sets off the introductory phrase, and a period correctly ends the sentence. No colons or apostrophes are needed in this sentence; *its* should be possessive, meaning it should have no apostrophe.

11. **C) is correct.** Choice C, *accommadations*, is spelled incorrectly. It should be spelled *accommodations*.

12. **A) is correct.** Choice A, *seige*, is spelled incorrectly. It should be spelled *siege*.

13. **D) is correct.** Choice D, *harrassing*, is spelled incorrectly. It should be spelled *harassing*.

14. **B) is correct.** Choice B, *noticably*, is spelled incorrectly. It should be spelled *noticeably*.

15. **C) is correct.** Choice C, *possesion*, is spelled incorrectly. It should be spelled *possession*.

INDUCTIVE REASONING

1. **A) is correct.** Both burglaries and robberies increase and peak at 12:00 a.m.

2. **C) is correct.** The sharpest decline in robberies and burglaries occurs between 12:00 a.m. and 2:00 a.m. The decline between 2:00 a.m. and 4:00 a.m. is not as dramatic.

3. **D) is correct.** While the number of burglaries plummets at 10:00 p.m., the number of robberies is still quite high, so the best answer is 6:00 a.m., when both crimes, on average, are at their lowest.

4. **A) is correct.** While the decrease in crime continues through 9:00 p.m., the graph shows that this trend begins at 8:00 p.m.

5. **D) is correct.** According to the graph, crime peaks around 12:00 a.m., which means that any time frame including 12:00 a.m. is incorrect. Crime is shown to decrease between 2:00 a.m. and 6:00 a.m.

6. **A) is correct.** According to the graph, the state police carried out close to eighty stops between January and March before climbing close to one hundred stops in April and May.

7. **C) is correct.** The graph shows that both the state police and municipal police had close to one hundred stops in April.

8. **D) is correct.** According to the graph, the state and municipal police issued nearly the same number of stops in February (approximately eighty) and April (approximately one hundred).

9. **D) is correct.** Stops reached a five-month high for state police in May, climbing to over one hundred.

10. **A) is correct.** Municipal police stops were at their lowest (below forty) in January.

11. **B) is correct.** The sharpest decrease occurs from July (the likely all-time high) to August.

12. **C) is correct.** The DUIs decreased from a high of one hundred to between seventy and eighty incidents. The best answer is a twenty-four–incident decrease. In October, there were only about seventy-five or seventy-six DUI incidents; 100 – 76 = 24.

13. **A) is correct.** There were one hundred DUI incidents in July, more than any other month.

14. **D) is correct.** October is the only month with fewer than eighty DUIs.

15. **C) is correct.** August and September have the closest data points, hovering close to eighty DUIs, while July and October are outliers.

DEDUCTIVE REASONING

1. **C) is correct.** The only rule followed was that the meeting took place in the chief's conference room. The meeting was not conducted at a reasonable hour; it was after an overnight shift. The officer's Statement of Rights was not read, the meeting and did not offer breaks, and the captain denied the officer the right to record the meeting.

2. **B) is correct.** The board did not read a Statement of Rights.

3. **A) is correct.** The board correctly followed all five steps of the State Code.

4. **B) is correct.** The range of disciplinary action for excessive loitering in the workplace is written warning to suspension.

5. **C) is correct.** The required disciplinary action for threatening to overthrow the government or joining an anti-government group is automatic discharge.

6. **B) is correct.** The range of disciplinary action for unauthorized use of a weapon is suspension to discharge.

7. **D) is correct.** The required disciplinary action for three consecutive absences

without administrative approval is compulsory resignation.

8. **A) is correct.** The range of disciplinary action for insubordination is written warning to suspension. Since this is Officer Gordon's first offense, he will likely receive a reprimand.

9. **B) is correct.** According to the rules and regulations, during an investigation, an employee will be placed on leave, but with pay.

10. **A) is correct.** According to the rules and regulations, "Whenever an agency member is suspended without pay, they may appeal this disciplinary action within one (1) month of their suspension."

11. **A) is correct.** According to the rules and regulations, "Whenever an agency member is demoted, they may appeal this disciplinary action within one (1) month of their demotion."

12. **B) is correct.** The last step Officer Morrison took was running the license plate to determine whether the car is stolen. Since the car is not stolen, the next step should be to contact the vehicle's owner(s).

13. **D) is correct.** Officer McNamara forgot to contact the vehicle's owner(s).

14. **D) is correct.** According to protocol, Officer White should carry out a field sobriety assessment to determine whether the individual is intoxicated.

15. **A) is correct.** Officer Del Rio "reserves the right to confiscate a driver's license if they refuse to take a blood alcohol test."

INFORMATION ORDERING

1. **A) is correct.** The most logical sequence is that the victim got off their shift, went for a walk on the boardwalk, was approached by the vagrant asking for money, refused the vagrant's request, and was assaulted as a result.

2. **B) is correct.** The first five events set up the assault and robbery: the victim rounds the corner, sees Daniel, and tries to not interact with him. Daniel responds by not letting her pass and grabbing her arm. This is the only logical order for these events because each step is consequential; each event is reliant upon the details of the previous event.

3. **A) is correct.** The assault and robbery must occur AFTER the five preceding events. Listing these events in reverse order would be illogical. The victim must run to the backyard before she can be chased there. She must be tackled before she can be on the ground. She must cry before she can be heard crying. And the neighbor must hear her before chasing Daniel away.

4. **A) is correct.** The person must be searched before they can be handcuffed. They must be handcuffed before they can be placed in the police cruiser. And they must be fully detained before it is safe enough to notify dispatch.

5. **B) is correct.** The two men must enter the gas station before they can commit the crime at gunpoint at the cash register. The cash must be requested before it is handed over. The police entered just as it was handed over, so their attempt to deter an escape would come after their entrance. The two men escaped just after the police told them to stop.

6. **C) is correct.** The couple must be arguing before they can get the attention of everyone in the bar. The woman's brother would have to hear the argument before he could monitor it and intervene. The brother would likely threaten to stab the man before actually stabbing him.

7. **C) is correct.** The older man would likely have to park the car and enter the school before the suspect in the red hooded sweatshirt could turn the corner and take advantage of the situation. The suspect would have to approach the car before he used the tool to break the window. The window had to be broken before the older man could hear it. He would likely have to come outside before he could yell at the young man.

8. **A) is correct.** Heart failure is more threatening than the other injuries. Deep wound bleeding is more life-threatening than shock but less life-threatening than a heart attack. A non-protruding broken bone is more dangerous than minor lacerations but not quite as urgent as shock, deep wound bleeding, and heart failure. Minor lacerations are typically not of high concern.

9. **A) is correct.** She would have to see the teenagers before asking them a question. The teenagers would have to be asked a question before it could be ignored. They would have to be in the alleyway before causing damage. The breaking glass and booming sound would likely occur before the smoke and flames. She would likely have to see the teens running off from the smoke and flames before calling 911.

10. **C) is correct.** The witnesses would have to see the fire from afar before they could see it up close. Once they got close, they would likely see the protesters with sledgehammers. The sledgehammers would have to break the statues' foundations before the statues began to collapse. And the witnesses would see the statues begin to collapse before they finally fell.

11. **C) is correct.** The passage states, "The police arrived just as the first statue tumbled to the ground. The protesters scattered." It is reasonable to infer that the police scared the protesters away; the statue was already collapsing and the fire was already raging.

12. **C) is correct.** Betty would have to enter the store first (at 3:00 a.m.). She would first obtain the milk before paying for it at the cash register. She had to have noticed the man before seeing him pull a gun. She would likely drop to the ground in response to seeing the gun.

13. **C) is correct.** She sees the men arguing before she sees Bruce get shoved. Bruce would have to be shoved first in order to fall and hit his head. The man exited the side door *after* the assault, so that would be after Bruce hit his head. And she does not call the police until *after* the man leaves.

14. **A) is correct.** The officer would have to register the firearms before entering the facility. The officer would then have to acquire the proper safety gear at the front desk. The officer would have to reach the firing area and fire before reloading. Equipment would be returned after all firing has been completed.

15. **D) is correct.** The masked criminals would have to enter the fast-food restaurant before requesting valuables. The valuables were stolen before the police officer entered. The individuals fled because of the police officer. And the victim would remain on scene to give a statement *after* this occurred.

PROBLEM SENSITIVITY

1. **C) is correct.** Officer Brown's restless, anxious, shaking, and erratic behaviors—combined with the dilated and bloodshot eyes and the apparent presence of pills without a prescription—are all signs of possible drug use.

2. **D) is correct.** Medication is usually provided in a prescription bottle or package. It is suspicious that Brown has a bag of pills that don't appear to have a prescription—especially since Brown tried to conceal the pills. It is possible that they are illicit.

3. **B) is correct.** It is most likely that Officer Brown apologized to Officer Singh to repair their relationship after being caught concealing pills.

4. **D) is correct.** Kelly Zicchardo "heard someone shout, 'Drop your weapon!' [and] remembers looking at the cash register, and it said 7:07 p.m."

5. **D) is correct.** Jim Lord is the only person, other than Harry Cartwright, to be in proximity of the crime.

6. **A) is correct.** The suspect is "known to be a local addict with a history of violence" and he already asked John Albright for "a fix or some cash."

7. **D) is correct.** The civilian might be the suspect, so it is important that Officer Crawley denies his requests to help but also engages him to uncover more information.

8. **C) is correct.** Both Jack Cho and Arnie Haynes saw a tall, young man running away from a fire scene.

9. **D) is correct.** Officer Gordon did not report the make and model of the vehicle.

10. **D) is correct.** The suspicious-looking person matches the description of the burglar, so it is best practice to stop the man to gain more insight.

11. **B) is correct.** The best approach would be to report this type of behavior to the commanding officer or another supervisor.

12. **C) is correct.** Witness 3's information does not match the details of the information provided by the other three witnesses.

13. **C) is correct.** Violations of protocol need to be reported, even in moments of emotional escalation. It is best to discuss the situation with your partner to maintain a productive working environment.

14. **C) is correct.** Hesitation could be fatal for the victim.

15. **A) is correct.** It is important to maintain all directives and protocols coming from supervisors.

SPATIAL ORIENTATION

1. **C) is correct.** Officer Willis will cross three intersections on his way to the bank from the police station.

2. **B) is correct.** Officer Willis will make two right-hand turns to get to the bank from the police station.

3. **B) is correct.** Officer Willis will cross the railroad tracks once on the way to the hospital from the library.

4. **A) is correct.** No left turns need to be made to get from the library to the hospital.

5. **C) is correct.** There is only one streetlight depicted on the map, but Officer Willis will pass it three times on his route.

6. **D) is correct.** On this patrol route, Officer Willis will cross the train tracks four times.

7. **B) is correct.** On this patrol route, Officer Willis will pass the bank a total of two times.

8. **C) is correct.** Officer Klinger will make two right-hand turns to get to the scene of the crash.

9. **A) is correct.** Officer Klinger will not have to make any left-hand turns.

10. **B) is correct.** On this route, Officer Klinger will make two turns.

11. **A) is correct.** Officer Klinger will be located on the northeast section of the map when she pulls over the car.

12. **A) is correct.** Officer Klinger will make one left-hand turn during the pursuit.

13. **A) is correct.** Officer Klinger will travel on one four-lane highway: Whitney Parkway.

14. **C) is correct.** There are thirteen residential streets designated on the map.

15. **C) is correct.** There are three highways: two four-lane highways and one two-lane highway.

MEMORIZATION

1. **B) is correct.** The suspect is wearing jeans and a hooded sweatshirt.

2. **D) is correct.** The subject is leaning against a squad car as one police officer frisks him.

3. **C) is correct.** The female police officer is holding onto handcuffs with her left hand.

4. **D) is correct.** There is a person (wearing black) lying on the ground in the upper left-hand corner of the photograph.

5. **B) is correct.** The officer is placing a marker labeled with the number *2* near the crime scene.

6. **B) is correct.** There is one person lying on the ground in the upper left-hand corner of the photo and there is also one officer.

7. **C) is correct.** The person in the photograph has a brush in their right hand.

8. **B) is correct.** There are two markers visible in the dirt.

9. **C) is correct.** The log, dirt, and plants most likely are part of a wooded area.

10. **C) is correct.** The handcuffs on the suspect indicate that the officer on the left is most likely detaining the suspect.

11. **C) is correct.** There is a traffic cone visible to the left of the suspect, through the officer's legs.

12. **C) is correct.** The suspect's face cannot be seen because it is facing away from the camera. It is not turned to the left or right.

13. **D) is correct.** The back of the officer's vest says "NYPD."

14. **A) is correct.** The car's front end is pointing to the left of the photo, indicating that it is most likely driving from right to left.

15. **C) is correct.** The officer is standing at an intersection, close to a crosswalk, indicating that he is likely directing traffic. The officer also has a traffic vest and gloves on.